WORKBOOK

Focus on GRAMMAR 2

FOURTH EDITION

Samuela Eckstut-Didier

ALWAYS LEARNING

FOCUS ON GRAMMAR 2: An Integrated Skills Approach, Fourth Edition Workbook

Copyright © 2012, 2006, 2000, 1995 by Pearson Education, Inc.
All rights reserved.

Pearson Education, Inc., 10 Bank Street, White Plains, NY 10606

Staff credits: The people who made up the *Focus on Grammar 2, Fourth Edition, Workbook* team, representing editorial, production, design, and manufacturing, are: Aerin Csigay, Christine Edmonds, Nancy Flaggman, Ann France, Stacey Hunter, Lise Minovitz, Robert Ruvo, and Marian Wassner.

Cover image: Shutterstock.com
Text composition: ElectraGraphics, Inc.
Text font: New Aster

Photo credit: **p. 58** David R. Frazier/Photolibrary, Inc.

Illustrations: **Steve Attoe:** p. 90; **ElectraGraphics, Inc.:** p. 18–19, 27, 32, 56, 57, 62, 86, 105, 115, 129, 143, 152, 154, 159, 166, 167, 174–175, 194; **Chris Gash:** pp. 84–85; **Dave Sullivan:** pp. 13, 121–122, 134–135; **Gary Torrisi:** p. 55

ISBN 10: 0-13-216349-7
ISBN 13: 978-0-13-216349-1

Printed in the United States of America

7 8 9 10—V001—16

Contents

ABOUT THE AUTHOR

Samuela Eckstut-Didier has taught ESL and EFL for over twenty-five years in the United States, Greece, Italy, and England. Currently she is teaching at Boston University, Center for English Language and Orientation Programs (CELOP). She has authored or co-authored numerous texts for the teaching of English, notably *Center Stage 2, 3,* and *4; Strategic Reading 1, 2,* and *3; What's in a Word? Reading and Vocabulary Building; In the Real World; First Impressions; Beneath the Surface; Widely Read;* and *Finishing Touches.*

UNIT 1 Present of *Be*: Statements

EXERCISE 1: Affirmative and Negative Statements with *Be*

Complete the sentences with **am, is,** *or* **are.**

1. Carrie Underwood ____is____ not from Brazil.

2. Lionel Messi _____ an Argentinean soccer player.

3. I _____ not a famous soccer player.

4. Soccer _____ popular in England.

5. Baseball and volleyball _____ sports.

6. Baseball _____ not the number one sport in Brazil.

7. Baseball players _____ from different countries.

8. Baseball _____ not my favorite sport.

9. Keira Knightley _____ not a soccer player.

10. I _____ a big soccer fan.

EXERCISE 2: Subject Pronouns

Change the underlined words. Use **he, she, it, we,** *or* **they.**

      Hello. I am Rocco. My last name is Marciano. ~~My last name~~ is an Italian name. My
                                     It
                                       1.

family and I are from Italy. Now <u>my family and I</u> live here. Anna is my mother. <u>My mother</u>
                                       2.   **3.**

is from a village in Abruzzi. <u>The village</u> is very small. Silvano is my father. <u>My father</u> is from
                                       4.   **5.**

Naples. <u>Naples</u> is a big city in the south of Italy. I am from Naples too.
          6.

      My parents are in Italy now. <u>My parents</u> are on vacation. I am at home with my sisters.
                                     7.

<u>My sisters and I</u> are not happy alone. <u>My sisters</u> are always angry with me. My brother is
  8.   **9.**

lucky. <u>My brother</u> is not at home. <u>My brother</u> is at college. <u>The college</u> is far away.
      10.   **11.**   **12.**

EXERCISE 3: Affirmative of *Be*

*Write true statements. Use words from columns **A**, **B**, and **C** in each sentence.*

A	B	C	
I			
My best friend		friendly	successful
My mother	am	happy	hardworking
My father	is	talented	a student
My teacher	are	from ___	an athlete
My parents		smart	funny
My classmates		busy	rich

1. *I am a student. I'm from Mexico.*

2. _____

3. _____

4. _____

5. _____

6. _____

7. _____

8. _____

9. _____

10. _____

EXERCISE 4: Negative Statements with *Be*

*Make the following sentences true by using **not**. Then write another sentence with the words in parentheses.*

1. Derek Jeter and Alex Rodriguez are singers. (athletes)

   Derek Jeter and Alex Rodriguez are not singers. They are athletes.

2. Gwyneth Paltrow is a tennis player. (actress)

   _____

3. Chris Martin is Gwyneth Paltrow's neighbor. (husband)

   _____

4. Chris Martin is an ice hockey player. (singer)

   _____

5. Dallas is a state. (city)

_____

6. California is a country. (state)

_____

7. Egypt and China are cities. (countries)

_____

8. Boston and New York are in Canada. (the United States)

_____

9. Ottawa is the capital of the United States. (Canada)

_____

10. Mexico is in Central America. (North America)

_____

EXERCISE 5: Affirmative and Negative Statements with *Be*

Complete the sentences. Use **is, is not, are,** *or* **are not.**

1. Apples _____ *are not* _____ black.

2. The Earth _____ round.

3. The sun _____ cold.

4. Cigarettes _____ good for you.

5. Lemons _____ yellow.

6. Cars _____ cheap.

7. Peter _____ a name.

8. An elephant _____ a small animal.

9. English, Spanish, and Arabic _____ languages.

10. The president of the United States _____ an astronaut.

EXERCISE 6: Contractions of Affirmative Statements with *Be*

Rewrite the conversations in full form.

1. A: Mario's a good volleyball player. *Mario is a good volleyball player.*

    B: Maria's good too. *Maria is good too.*

2. A: We're from New York. _____

    B: I'm from New York too. _____

3. A: I'm a big baseball fan. _____

    B: I'm not. _____

4. A: Jessica's a very good soccer player. _____

    B: She's a good student too. _____

5. A: You're Mark, right? _____

    B: No, I'm not Mark. I'm his brother Mike. _____

6. A: Pedro's nineteen. _____

    B: No, he's not. He's sixteen. _____

7. A: Basketball's a popular sport. Soccer's popular too. _____

    _____

    B: They're not popular in my country. _____

EXERCISE 7: Contractions of Affirmative and Negative Statements with *Be*

Rewrite the conversations with contractions.

1. A: Mario is a good volleyball player. *Mario's a good volleyball player.*

    B: Maria is good too. *Maria's good too.*

2. A: Yung-Hee and Ali are not in class today. _____

    B: They are at a game. _____

3. A: The teacher is not in class. _____

    B: I know. She is sick. _____

4. A: Antonio is a student in your class. _____

    B: His name is not on my list. _____

5. A: Melinda is successful. _____

    B: She is pretty too. _____

6. A: I am right. _____

    B: No, you are not. You are wrong. _____

7. A: They are my books. _____

    B: No, they are not. They are my books. _____

EXERCISE 8: Editing

Correct the paragraph. There are seven mistakes. The first mistake is already corrected.
Find and correct six more.

                      is

My favorite sport ~~are~~ baseball. It be popular in the United States. My favorite players are

Felix Hernandez and Hanley Ramirez. Are baseball players in the United States. But they

not from the United States. Felix Hernandez he is from Venezuela. Hanley Ramirez is no

from Venezuela. He from the Dominican Republic.

EXERCISE 9: Personal Writing

Write sentences about your favorite sport, team, or player. Use the words from the box
to help you.

> My favorite sport / team / player is . . .
>
> His / Her name is . . .
>
> He / She is / isn't . . .
>
> He's / She's from . . .

_____

_____

_____

_____

Present of *Be*: *Yes / No* Questions and *Wh-* Questions

EXERCISE 1: Affirmative Statements and Questions with *Be*

*Put a question mark (**?**) at the end of each question. Put a period (**.**) at the end of each sentence.*

1. It is December 15th .

2. Is it December 15th ?

3. Are we in the right classroom __

4. Why are you and your classmates unhappy __

5. Who is your teacher __

6. We are very good students __

7. I am from Florida __

8. Is your watch expensive __

9. Where is Michigan __

10. Are the students from the same country __

11. Is your car comfortable __

12. This exercise is easy __

EXERCISE 2: *Yes / No* Questions and Short Answers with *Be*

Match the questions and answers.

__d__ 1. Is Preeda from Thailand?

____ 2. Are Pat and Tom American?

____ 3. Are you Lucy Simone?

____ 4. Are you ready?

____ 5. Is the doctor in the office?

____ 6. Are Mr. and Mrs. Saris here?

____ 7. Is the TV in the living room?

____ 8. Is John married?

____ 9. Is the book good?

____ 10. Are you students at King High School?

____ 11. Is your mother home?

____ 12. Are you and the other students happy in this class?

a. Yes, she is. She's in the kitchen with my father.

b. Yes, we are. Our teacher's wonderful.

c. Yes, they are. They're in the garden.

d. Yes, he is. He's from Bangkok.

e. No, we aren't. We're students at Kennedy High School.

f. No, they're not. They're British.

g. No, it isn't. It's in the bedroom.

h. No, I'm not. I'm Anna Sanchez.

i. Yes, it is. It's very interesting.

j. No, I'm not. Please wait a minute.

k. Yes, he is. His wife's a detective.

l. Yes, she is. She's with a patient.

EXERCISE 3: *Yes / No* Questions and Short Answers with *Be*

Put the words in the correct order. Write questions. Then write true short answers.

1. the teacher / you / Are

   Are you the teacher? _____   No, I'm not. _____

2. you / Are / happy

   _____   _____

3. a student / your mother / Is

   _____   _____

4. today / Is / Thursday

   _____   _____

5. Are / from California / your friends

   _____   _____

6. talented / your friend / Is

   _____   _____

(continued on next page)

7. a singer / Are / you

_____ _____

8. your teacher / Is / friendly

_____ _____

9. your mother and father / Canadian / Are

_____ _____

10. Are / married / you

_____ _____

11. young / your classmates / Are

_____ _____

12. it / Is / eleven o'clock

_____ _____

EXERCISE 4: *Wh-* Questions and Answers with *Be*

Put the words in the correct order. Write questions. Then answer the questions with the answers from the box.

A sandwich.	~~My mother.~~
~~At home.~~	On Park Street.
It's great!	Shakespeare.
Because she's tired.	I'm your new teacher.
Brazil.	On Saturday.

1. are / parents / Where / your

Where are your parents?   At home.

2. in / is / car / the / Who

Who is in the car?   My mother.

3. from / Where / they / are

_____ _____

4. in bed / your mother / Why / is

_____ _____

5. bag / is / the / What / in

_____ _____

6. post office / the / is / Where

_____ _____

7. Who / your / writer / favorite / is

_____ _____

8. English class / How / your / is

_____ _____

9. class trip / is / When / the

_____ _____

10. you / Why / here / are

_____ _____

EXERCISE 5: Question Words

Complete the sentences. Use **who, what, why,** or **where.** Remember to add the correct capitalization.

DAD: _____ What _____ 's this?
                    1.

LAURA: It's a painting.

DAD: I know that. _____'s it here in the kitchen?
                          2.

LAURA: I don't know. It's not my painting. It's Mike's painting.

DAD: By the way, _____'s Mike?
                         3.

LAURA: At the museum.

DAD: At the museum? Your brother? _____'s he at the museum?
                                          4.

LAURA: Because his friend is there.

DAD: _____'s his friend's name?
              5.

LAURA: Ratana.

DAD: _____'s Ratana?
              6.

LAURA: Mike's girlfriend.

DAD: Mike's girlfriend?

(continued on next page)

LAURA: Uh-huh.

DAD: Ratana's an unusual name. _____'s she from?

7.

LAURA: Dad, I don't know. She's not my girlfriend.

EXERCISE 6: *Wh-* Questions

Write the questions. Use **how, who, what, why,** *or* **where.** *Remember to add the correct capitalization.*

1. **A:** _Who is he?_ OR _Who's he?_____

   B: He's one of the students in my English class.

2. **A:** _____

   B: The hospital? It's on Porter Street.

3. **A:** _____

   B: Javier Bardem? He is an actor.

4. **A:** _____

   B: Room 203 . . . Room 203. I'm sorry. I don't know.

5. **A:** _____

   B: I think your keys are on the TV.

6. **A:** _____

   B: On the phone? It's a friend from school.

7. **A:** _____

   B: Cadillacs are cars.

8. **A:** _____

   B: That? It's my smart phone.

9. **A:** _____

   B: The wastepaper basket is next to the desk.

10. **A:** _____

    B: My parents? They're fine.

Correct the conversation. There are nine mistakes. The first mistake is already corrected. Find and correct eight more.

CLAUDIA: Excuse me. ~~This is~~ *Is this* Room 202?

TEACHER: Yes, it's.

ENRIQUE: Oh. We late for class?

TEACHER: No, you're right on time.

ENRIQUE: That's good!

TEACHER: So, what your names? You are Ana Leite and Fernando Romeiro from Brazil?

CLAUDIA: No, we're are not. I'm Claudia **Rodriguez**. And this is Enrique Montero.

TEACHER: Where you are from?

CLAUDIA: We're from Venezuela.

TEACHER: Hmm . . . your names are not on my list. **Are you in English 4?**

CLAUDIA: No, I don't think. I think we're in **English 2.**

TEACHER: Then this is not your class. **You're in Room 302.**

CLAUDIA: Who the teacher is?

TEACHER: I'm not sure.

A. *Complete the sentences with true answers.*

I'm from _____.

My email address is _____.

My English class is _____.

My class is on _____.

The teacher's name is _____.

(continued on next page)

B. *Imagine you are going to be an "email friend" with someone in an English class in another country. Write questions for the statements on the previous page.*

_____

_____

_____

_____

_____

Past of *Be*: Statements, *Yes / No* Questions, *Wh-* Questions

EXERCISE 1: Past of *Be*: Affirmative and Negative Statements

A. *Complete Jack's statements about his last job. Use* **was** *or* **were**.

1. "I _____ was _____ on time for work every day."

2. "My work _____ perfect."

3. "My co-workers _____ sad when I left."

4. "My customers _____ happy with my work."

5. "I _____ very hardworking."

B. *Change the positive statements to negative ones. Then use the information in parentheses to make true statements about Jack.*

1. Jack was on time every day. (late) → _Jack was not on time every day. He was late!_

2. His work was perfect. (terrible) → _____

3. His co-workers were sad when he left. (happy) → _____

4. His customers were happy with his work. (unhappy) → _____

5. He was hardworking. (lazy) → _____

EXERCISE 2: Past of *Be*: Affirmative and Negative Statements

Write sentences. Use **was, wasn't, were,** *or* **weren't.**

1. Abraham Lincoln / born / in England

Abraham Lincoln's wasn't born in England.

2. Picasso and Michelangelo / painters

Picasso and Michelangelo were painters.

3. William Shakespeare and Charles Dickens / Canadian

4. Barack Obama / the first president of the United States

5. Charlie Chaplin and Marilyn Monroe / movie stars

6. The end of World War I / in 1942

7. *Titanic* / the name of a movie

8. Toronto and Washington, D.C. / big cities 300 years ago

9. Indira Gandhi and Napoleon / famous people

10. Nelson Mandela / a political leader

11. Oregon and Hawaii / part of the United States / in 1776

12. Disneyland / a famous place / 100 years ago

Put the words in the correct order. Then answer the questions.

1. your mother / at home / Was / last night / ? <u>Was your mother at home</u>

<u>last night? Yes, she was.</u> OR <u>No, she wasn't.</u>

2. Were / a student / 10 years ago / you / ? _____

_____

3. you / in English class / yesterday / Were / ? _____

_____

4. all the students / last week / Were / in class / ? _____

_____

5. the weather / Was / yesterday / nice / ? _____

_____

6. at work / Was / two days ago / your teacher / ? _____

_____

EXERCISE 4: Past of *Be*: *Wh-* Questions

*Write questions with **how, what, when**, or **where** and **was** or **were**.*

1. A: My first job was in a bookstore. <u>Where was your first job?</u>

   B: In a drugstore.

2. A: I was a cashier. _____

   B: I was a cashier too.

3. A: My store was downtown. _____

   B: It was near my home.

4. A: My job was pretty boring. _____

   B: It was fun.

5. A: My co-workers weren't very friendly. _____

   B: They were nice.

6. A: I was at the bookstore every weekend. _____

   B: I was at the drugstore every day after school.

EXERCISE 5: *Be*: Present and Past

Complete the conversation. Use **is, are, was,** *or* **were.** *Remember to add the correct capitalization.*

A: It _____is_____ a beautiful day.
     1.

B: Yes, it is—especially because the weather _____was_____ so terrible yesterday. The weather
                                              2.

in this city _____ so strange. One day it _____ warm, and the next day it
            3.   **4.**

_____ cold.
5.

A: You _____ right about that. In my country, it _____ always warm and sunny.
       6.   **7.**

The beaches are always crowded!

B: _____ it warm in the winter too?
   8.

A: Uh-huh. It _____ usually between 70 and 90 degrees. Last Christmas I _____
              9.   **10.**

home for two weeks, and it _____ sunny and warm. My friends and I _____ at
                        11.   **12.**

the beach every day. How about you? _____ you here this past Christmas?
                                  13.

B: Yeah. My parents _____ here for five days for a visit. We _____ cold most of
                    14.   **15.**

the time, and my mother _____ ill for a few days. They _____ happy to see me,
                      16.   **17.**

but they _____ glad to leave this awful weather.
       18.

A: _____ your parents back home now?
   19.

B: No, they _____ on another vacation—this time, in a warm place.
             20.

EXERCISE 6: Editing

Correct the conversation. There are six mistakes. The first mistake is already corrected.
Find and correct five more.

    was your first day in class
A: So how ~~your first day in class was~~?

B: It weren't too good at first.

A: What is wrong?

B: First, I no was in the right classroom. Two other students was in the wrong classroom

too. The class was boring. Everything was so difficult.

A: How long you there?

B: For half an hour.

Write about your first day in English class.

EXAMPLE: The first day of English class was on October 1st. It was a warm, sunny day. It was a beautiful day to go to the park with friends, so I wasn't very happy about English class. But the teacher was friendly, and some of the students in the class were friends from last year's class, so I was happy. Class was fun that day.

_____

_____

_____

_____

PART II

NOUNS, ADJECTIVES, PREPOSITIONS

UNIT 4 **Count Nouns and Proper Nouns**

EXERCISE 1: Nouns

Look at the pictures. Unscramble the letters to make words.

1. rac   <u>c</u> <u>a</u> <u>r</u>

2. wrofles   <u>f</u> <u>l</u> <u>o</u> <u>w</u> <u>e</u> <u>r</u> <u>s</u>

3. thoscel   __ <u>l</u> __ __ __ __ __

4. shotop   <u>P</u> __ __ __ __ __ __

5. labelurm   <u>u</u> __ __ <u>r</u> __ __ __

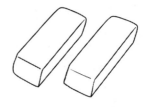

6. arseers   <u>e</u> __ <u>a</u> __ __ __ __

7. rossicss   <u>s</u> <u>c</u> __ __ __ __ __ __

J	A	N	U	A	R	Y
New Year's Day 1	2	3				
7	8	9	10			

8. loyihad   <u>h</u> __ __ __ __ __ __ <u>y</u>

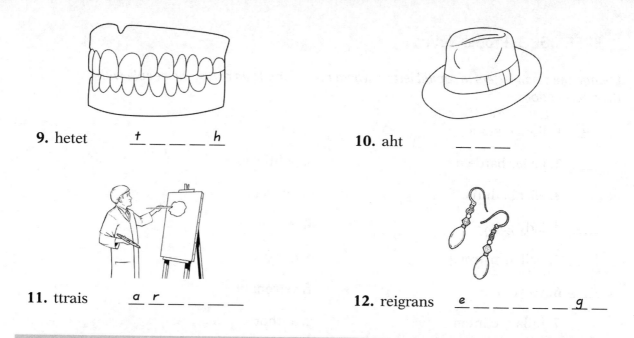

9. hetet   <u>t</u> <u> </u> <u> </u> <u> </u> <u>h</u>

10. aht   <u> </u> <u> </u> <u> </u>

11. ttrais   <u>a</u> <u>r</u> <u> </u> <u> </u> <u> </u> <u> </u>

12. reigrans   <u>e</u> <u> </u> <u> </u> <u> </u> <u> </u> <u> </u> <u>g</u> <u> </u>

EXERCISE 2: Singular and Plural Nouns

Write sentences for the words in Exercise 1. Use **it's** *for singular nouns and* **they're** *for plural nouns. Add* **a** *or* **an** *where necessary.*

1. <u>It's a car.</u>

2. <u>They're flowers.</u>

3. _____

4. _____

5. _____

6. _____

7. _____

8. _____

9. _____

10. _____

11. _____

12. _____

EXERCISE 3: Proper Nouns

Change the small letters to capital letters where necessary. Then match the people with their occupations.

           L   M

_d_ 1. lionel messi   **a.** actor

____ 2. javier bardem   **b.** politician

____ 3. elizabeth II   **c.** musician

____ 4. lady gaga   **d.** athlete

____ 5. neil armstrong   **e.** queen

____ 6. yo-yo ma   **f.** astronaut

____ 7. hillary clinton   **g.** author

____ 8. j. k. rowling   **h.** singer

EXERCISE 4: Nouns with *A / An*

Write sentences about the people in Exercise 3.

1. _Lionel Messi is an athlete._ _____

2. _____

3. _____

4. _____

5. _____

6. _____

7. _____

8. _____

EXERCISE 5: Plural Nouns

Say these plural nouns. Then write them in the correct columns.

boxes	classes	girls	notebooks	states
~~boys~~	dictionaries	houses	roommates	students
~~carrots~~	~~dresses~~	lemons	sons	watches

/s/	/z/	/ɪz/
carrots	boys	dresses
_____	_____	_____
_____	_____	_____
_____	_____	_____
_____	_____	_____

EXERCISE 6: Plural Nouns

Complete the sentences. Use the plural form of the words from the box.

actor	city	country	man	river	state	watch
~~cat~~	continent	holiday	mountain	song	university	~~woman~~

1. Toyotas and Fords are _____ cars _____.

2. Mrs. Robb and Ms. Hernandez are _____ women _____.

3. Mr. Katz and John Mallin are _____.

4. "A Hard Day's Night" and "Happy Birthday to You" are _____.

5. London and Cairo are _____.

6. The Nile and the Amazon are _____.

7. Asia and Africa are _____.

8. Florida and Michigan are _____.

9. Brazil and Kenya are _____.

10. Thanksgiving and Christmas are _____.

11. Harvard and Yale are _____.

12. Seikos and Rolexes are _____.

(continued on next page)

13. Nicole Kidman and Gwyneth Paltrow are _____.

14. The Himalayas and the Alps are _____.

Write the singular or plural form of the nouns.

1. 4 women
   + 1 ___woman___
   ‾‾‾‾‾‾‾‾‾‾‾‾‾‾‾‾‾
   5 ___women___

2. 1 child
   + 2 _____
   ‾‾‾‾‾‾‾‾‾‾‾‾‾‾‾‾‾
   3 _____

3. 1 tooth
   + 6 _____
   ‾‾‾‾‾‾‾‾‾‾‾‾‾‾‾‾‾
   7 _____

4. 3 feet
   + 1 _____
   ‾‾‾‾‾‾‾‾‾‾‾‾‾‾‾‾‾
   4 _____

5. 6 grandchildren
   + 1 _____
   ‾‾‾‾‾‾‾‾‾‾‾‾‾‾‾‾‾
   7 _____

6. 8 people
   + 1 _____
   ‾‾‾‾‾‾‾‾‾‾‾‾‾‾‾‾‾
   9 _____

7. 1 sister-in-law
   + 2 _____
   ‾‾‾‾‾‾‾‾‾‾‾‾‾‾‾‾‾
   3 _____

EXERCISE 8: Editing

*Correct the paragraph. There are six mistakes. The first mistake is already corrected.
Find and correct five more.*

　　　　　　 a
This is photo of me and my sister. Isn't she striking? She's architect. She lives in miami

with her husband and two childs. He's a dentists. In this photo, my sister and I are at a

special party for our parent.

EXERCISE 9: Personal Writing

*Describe a photo of you with other people. Use the paragraph in Exercise 8 as an
example.*

_____

_____

_____

_____

Descriptive Adjectives

Write the opposites of the underlined words.

1. A: Is the village <u>clean</u>?

   B: Yes, but the beaches are _____*dirty*_____.

2. A: Is the exercise <u>easy</u>?

   B: Yes, but the next one is _____.

3. A: Is the book <u>interesting</u>?

   B: Yes, but the movie is _____.

4. A: Are the restaurants <u>cheap</u>?

   B: Yes, but the hotels are _____.

5. A: Are the parks <u>dangerous</u>?

   B: Yes, but the streets are _____.

6. A: Is the hotel <u>big</u>?

   B: Yes, but the rooms are _____.

7. A: Is the bed <u>uncomfortable</u>?

   B: Yes, but the chair is _____.

8. A: Are the paintings <u>beautiful</u>?

   B: Yes, but the photos are _____.

9. A: Are the women <u>young</u>?

   B: Yes, but the men are _____.

10. A: Are your feet <u>cold</u>?

   B: Yes, but my hands are _____.

EXERCISE 2: Adjectives and Nouns

Combine the two sentences into one sentence.

1. They are actors. They are talented.

   They are talented actors.

2. It is a movie. It is long.

   _____

3. The Prado is a museum. The Prado is famous.

   _____

4. You are a photographer. You are unusual.

   _____

5. They are buildings. They are interesting.

   _____

6. He is a man. He is intelligent.

   _____

7. It is a village. It is crowded.

   _____

8. She is a soccer player. She is popular.

   _____

9. We are students. We are good.

   _____

10. This is an exercise. This is easy.

    _____

EXERCISE 3: *A / An*: Adjectives and Nouns

*Complete the sentences about your hometown. Circle the correct verb and write it on the first line. Add **a** or **an** on the second line where necessary.*

1. My hometown _____*is* OR *isn't*_____ ___*an*___ old city.

(is / isn't)

2. It _____ _____ famous.

(is / isn't)

3. It _____ _____ awesome place.

(is / isn't)

4. The people _____ _____ friendly.
(are / aren't)

5. The buildings _____ _____ unusual.
(are / aren't)

6. It _____ _____ expensive city.
(is / isn't)

7. It _____ _____ crowded place.
(is / isn't)

8. There _____ _____ beautiful park.
(is / isn't)

EXERCISE 4: Editing

Correct the mistake in each sentence. Then write correct sentences.

1. Those houses are comfortables.

Those houses are comfortable.

2. They are carpets beautiful.

_____

3. Those hotels are expensives.

_____

4. They are men honest.

_____

5. They are talls girls.

_____

6. Eggs are whites or brown.

_____

7. They are actors good.

_____

8. These watches are cheaps.

_____

9. They are stories interesting.

_____

10. The summers are hots and dry.

_____

Write about your hometown.

EXAMPLE: *I'm from Philadelphia. It's a big city on the east coast of the United States between New York and Washington, D.C. The average winter temperature is 42°F, and the average summer temperature is 83°F. The museums are terrific, and Philadelphia is an important city in American history.*

_____

_____

_____

_____

Prepositions of Place

EXERCISE 1: Prepositions of Place

Draw a picture of each sentence.

1. A cat is under a chair.

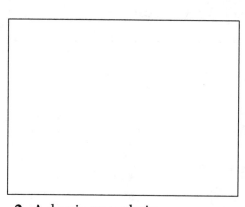

2. A dog is on a chair.

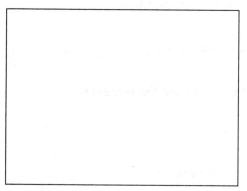

3. The glasses are near the book.

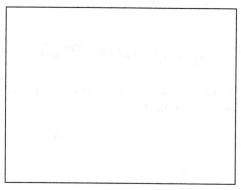

4. A man is in back of a chair.

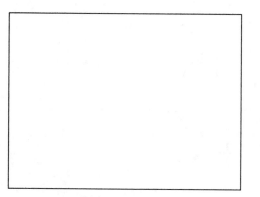

5. An apple is next to a banana.

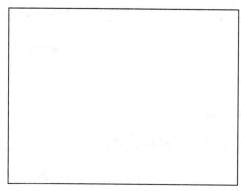

6. A woman is behind a little girl.

(continued on next page)

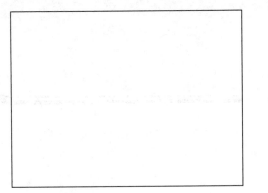

7. A ball is under a car.

8. Some flowers are between two trees.

9. A bicycle is in front of a house.

10. Two balls are in a box.

EXERCISE 2: Prepositions of Place

Look at the map in Appendix 2, page A-2 of your Student Book. Complete the sentences.
*Use **near**, **between**, **next to**, or **in**.*

1. Seattle is _____ *in* _____ Washington.

2. Saskatchewan is _____ Manitoba and Alberta.

3. Pennsylvania is _____ New Jersey.

4. Maine is _____ Massachusetts.

5. Halifax is _____ Nova Scotia.

6. Kansas is _____ Arkansas and Iowa.

7. Indiana is _____ Ohio and Illinois.

8. Prince Edward Island is _____ Canada.

9. Idaho is _____ Oregon.

10. Ottawa is _____ Montreal.

Complete the conversation. Use **in**, **on**, *or* **at**.

A: Where's your home?

B: _____In_____ Canada.
   1.

A: Where _____ Canada?
              2.

B: _____ Vancouver.
   3.

A: Where _____ Vancouver?
              4.

B: _____ Hastings Street.
   5.

A: Where _____ Hastings Street?
              6.

B: _____ 526 Hastings Street.
   7.

A: Is your apartment _____ the first floor or the second floor?
                         8.

B: It's _____ the twenty-third floor.
        9.

A: Oh. So is your home _____ a big apartment building?
                          10.

B: Very big.

Correct the conversation. There are six mistakes. The first mistake is already corrected.
Find and correct five more.

A: Where are you?

B: Near ✗ the ABC Movie Theater.

A: At Water Avenue?

B: Yeah, the corner Water Avenue and Park Street. Where are you?

A: I'm on the museum. It's right next of City Hall.

B: Oh, OK. Where in the museum?

A: In the second floor, between the cafeteria and the stairs, in front of the sculpture

exhibit.

EXERCISE 5: Personal Writing

Someone is going to meet you after your English class. Describe where your school is.

EXAMPLE: The school is on Market Street near 16th Street. It's in a small building between Central Bank and Dino's Restaurant. My class is on the third floor between the stairs and the rest room. It's Room 304. I'll meet you there.

_____

_____

_____

_____

_____

PART III

IMPERATIVES AND THE
SIMPLE PRESENT

UNIT 7 Imperatives; Suggestions with *Let's,*
Why don't we . . . ?

EXERCISE 1: Imperatives: Affirmative and Negative

A. *Match the people with their statements.*

   d   **1.** The teacher said,   **a.** "Leave me alone."

_____ **2.** Mr. Michaels told his children,   **b.** "Open your mouth and say, 'Ah.'"

_____ **3.** The doctor said,   **c.** "Put your hands up."

_____ **4.** The police officer said,   **d͞.** "Open your books to page 34."

_____ **5.** Jenny told her brother,   **e.** "Go to bed."

B. *Then do the same with these statements.*

_____ **6.** The teacher said,   **f.** "Don't move."

_____ **7.** Mr. Michaels told his children,   **g.** "Don't eat so fast."

_____ **8.** The doctor said,   **h.** "Don't bother me."

_____ **9.** The police officer said,   **i.** "Don't take a nap in class."

_____ **10.** Jenny told her brother,   **j.** "Don't take this medicine at night."

EXERCISE 2: Imperatives: Affirmative and Negative

*Complete the sentences. Use the verbs from the box. Add **don't** where necessary.*

ask	buy	give	~~open~~	talk	touch
be	clean	~~go~~	study	tell	use

1. I'm hot. Please _____*open*_____ the window.

2. That animal is dangerous. _____*Don't go*_____ near it.

3. _____ your room right now. It's a mess.

4. The baby is asleep. _____ so loudly.

5. The apples look bad. _____ them.

6. We're lost. _____ the police officer for directions.

(continued on next page)

7. It's a surprise party. _____ late.

8. This is a secret. _____ anyone.

9. The test is on Monday. _____ pages 50 and 51.

10. I'm cold. _____ me my sweater, please.

11. This glass isn't yours. _____ it.

12. The stove is hot. _____ it.

EXERCISE 3: Imperatives: Affirmative

Look at the map and complete the note. Use the verbs from the box.

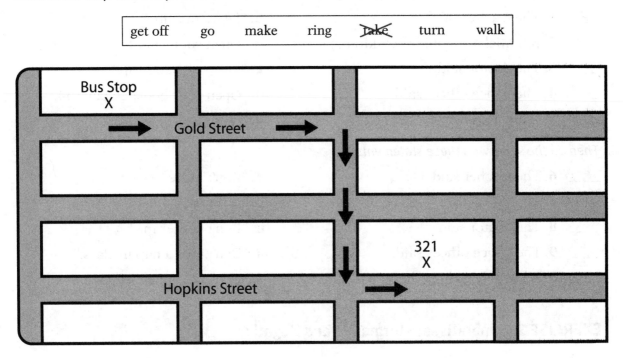

get off	go	make	ring	~~Take~~	turn	walk

DIRECTIONS

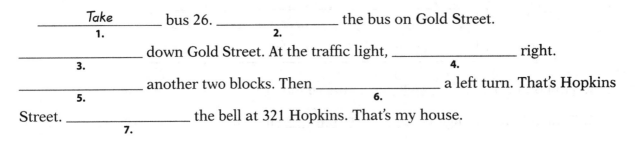

____Take____ bus 26. _____ the bus on Gold Street.
    1.   **2.**

_____ down Gold Street. At the traffic light, _____ right.
        3.   **4.**

_____ another two blocks. Then _____ a left turn. That's Hopkins
        5.   **6.**

Street. _____ the bell at 321 Hopkins. That's my house.
            7.

Complete the sentences. Circle the correct answers and write them on the lines.

1. Students in an English class say to the teacher, "_____Let's take a break._____"

   (a.) Let's take a break.

   b. Let's take a test.

2. Donny says to his brother, "_____"

   a. Why don't we clean our room?

   b. Why don't we play basketball?

3. It's Saturday night, and Eric and Sylvia Chiu are tired. Sylvia says,

   "_____"

   a. Let's go dancing tonight.

   b. Let's not do anything tonight.

4. It's five o'clock. One secretary says to another secretary,

   "_____"

   a. Why don't we go out for dinner?

   b. Why don't we work late tonight?

5. Two tourists are on an island. One tourist says to the other,

   "_____"

   a. Why don't we go to a beach?

   b. Why don't we stay in the hotel all day?

6. Louisa thinks TV is boring. She says to her boyfriend,

   "_____"

   a. Let's not watch TV tonight.

   b. Let's watch TV tonight.

7. It's a beautiful day. Miriam says to her roommate,

   "_____"

   a. Let's not forget our umbrellas.

   b. Let's not take the car to class today. Let's walk.

(continued on next page)

8. It's Frederico's birthday. His wife says to their daughter,

"_____"

   a. Why don't we get a present for Dad?

   b. Why don't we forget about Dad's birthday?

9. Celia and her sister are late. Celia says,

"_____"

   a. Let's take a taxi.

   b. Let's walk.

10. It's cold. Jenny says to her boyfriend,

"_____"

   a. Let's wait outside.

   b. Let's not wait outside.

EXERCISE 5: _Let's_ and _Why don't we . . . ?_

A. Write sentences. Use let's and the expressions from the box.

get something to eat	go swimming	leave
go inside	~~go to bed~~	not invite her to the party
go out and look for him		

  1. A: I'm tired.

    B: I am too.

    A: _Let's go to bed._

  2. A: I'm hungry.

    B: I am too.

    A: _____

  3. A: I'm hot.

    B: I am too.

    A: _____

4. A: I'm angry with Mariana.

   B: I am too.

   A: _____

B. *Write sentences. Use* **Why don't we . . . ?** *and the expressions from the box.*

5. A: I'm worried about Rocky. Where is he?

   B: I don't know.

   A: _____

6. A: I'm cold.

   B: I am too.

   A: _____

7. A: I'm bored at this party.

   B: I am too.

   A: _____

EXERCISE 6: *Why don't you . . . ?*

A. *Match the sentences and responses.*

   __c__ **1.** I'm tired.

   _____ **2.** I don't know the meaning of this word.

   _____ **3.** I don't know what to do tonight.

   _____ **4.** I'm hungry.

   _____ **5.** I'm hot.

   a. Why don't you make a sandwich?

   b. Why don't you go to the movies?

   c. Why don't you go to bed?

   d. Why don't you open the window?

   e. Why don't you look it up in the dictionary?

B. *Write your own responses with* **Why don't you . . . ?**

6. I'm bored.

_____

7. I want to practice English more.

_____

8. I have a headache.

_____

Complete the conversations. Use the words from the box.

can't	~~idea~~	it	plan	Sounds	Why
don't	instead	OK	Sorry	~~That's~~	

1. **A:** Let's go to the movies.

   B: _____That's_____ a good _____idea_____.

2. **A:** Why don't we go out for dinner?

   B: No, I _____ feel like _____.

3. **A:** Let's go to a Chinese restaurant for lunch.

   B: _____ don't we go to a Mexican restaurant _____?

4. **A:** Let's go to New York for a few days.

   B: _____, I _____. I'm really busy at work.

5. **A:** Let's stay at home tonight.

   B: _____.

6. **A:** Why don't we visit your sister and her family next weekend?

   B: Sounds like a _____.

7. **A:** Let's not take a taxi.

   B: _____ good to me. I like to walk.

EXERCISE 8: Editing

Correct the conversation. There are six mistakes. The first mistake is already corrected.
Find and correct five more.

     Let's
A: ~~Let~~ go for a walk. It's a beautiful afternoon.

B: That's a good idea. Why not we walk to Fireside and get something to eat?

A: Which restaurants are open there in the afternoon?

B: I don't know. You look online, but not take a long time. I'm ready to go.

A: How about Chico's?

B: That sounds good. But let's to call first. They're usually crowded.

A: OK. You are give me the phone.

EXERCISE 9: Personal Writing

Write advice for a happy life. Include at least five to six tips.

EXAMPLE: 1. Make a lot of friends.
2. Don't worry about small things.

_____

_____

_____

_____

_____

EXERCISE 1: Simple Present: Affirmative Statements

Read the job descriptions. Answer the questions. Use the words from the box.

cook	flight attendant	pilot	~~salesperson~~
doctor	mechanic	professor	secretary

1. I work in a store. I sell clothes. What am I?

   You're a salesperson.

2. Dina and Paul answer telephones and type letters. They work in a college office. What are they?

   _____

3. Captain Phillips goes to the airport every day. He flies airplanes. What is he?

   _____

4. Kay Williams gives lectures and meets with students. She works in a university. What is she?

   _____

5. Ben and Rachel work on an airplane. They serve meals and drinks to passengers. What are they?

   _____

6. I work in a restaurant. I prepare the food. What am I?

   _____

7. Daniel fixes cars. He works in a garage. What is he?

   _____

8. Ellen helps sick people. She works in a hospital. What is she?

   _____

Complete each sentence with the correct verb. Use the simple present form.

1. Mary is a taxi driver. She _____drives_____ a taxi.

2. Stuart is a Spanish teacher. He _____ Spanish.

3. Maria Domingo is a singer. She _____.

4. Nassos Morona is a dancer. He _____.

5. Bill Bright is a baseball player. He _____ baseball.

6. Shirley Simpson is a bank manager. She _____ a bank.

7. Sam and Victor are trash collectors. They _____ trash.

8. Margaret and Phil are house painters. They _____ houses.

9. Lou is a window washer. He _____ windows.

10. Oscar, Tom, and Steve are firefighters. They _____ fires.

Complete the conversation. Use the correct form of the verbs in parentheses.

A: Tell me about you and your family.

B: My husband and I _____are_____ pretty traditional. I _____ care of
              1. (be)   2. (take)
    the home, and he _____ to work. He _____ a business in
                            3. (go)   4. (have)
    town, but we _____ in an old house in the country.
                        5. (live)

A: Alone?

B: Oh, no. We _____ alone. We _____ six children—five
                        6. (not live)   7. (have)
    boys and one girl. Two of them _____ with us anymore. Our daughter
                                              8. (not live)
    _____ married, and she _____ with her family. She
          9. (be)   10. (live)
    _____ two children. One of our sons _____ also married,
          11. (have)   12. (be)
    but he _____ any children. Our other four sons _____ with
                  13. (not have)   14. (live)
    us. One of them, Peter, _____ at the local college and _____
                                  15. (study)   16. (work)
    part time at a company near the college. He _____ home every
                                                        17. (leave)
    morning at around six o'clock and _____ home until seven or eight
                                                18. (not come)

(continued on next page)

in the evening. It _____ a good schedule at all. Our son Russell
                       19. (not be)

_____ my husband. The other boys _____ teenagers; they
    20. (help)   **21. (be)**

_____ to high school. Charlie _____ a senior.
    22. (go)   **23. (be)**

A: Are you busy all the time?

B: Oh, yes. I _____ much free time at all. That's why we _____
                      24. (not have)   **25. (try)**

to rest on Sundays. We _____ up until nine o'clock.
                          26. (not get)

EXERCISE 4: Simple Present: Affirmative and Negative Statements

Correct the sentences. Use words from the box.

a big population	grass	the sun
during the day	mice	0° C
~~in the east~~	Antarctic	100° C
a hot climate	sand	big ears

1. The sun rises in the west.

   The sun doesn't rise in the west. It rises in the east.

2. Water boils at 90° C.

   _____

3. Water freezes at 5° C.

   _____

4. The Earth goes around the moon.

   _____

5. Penguins come from the Arctic.

   _____

6. Cows eat meat.

   _____

7. China has a small population.

_____

8. Deserts have a lot of water.

_____

9. Elephants have small ears.

_____

10. Egypt has a cold climate.

_____

11. The sun shines at night.

_____

12. Cats run after dogs.

_____

EXERCISE 5: Editing

Correct the conversation. There are eight mistakes. The first mistake is already corrected. Find and correct seven more.

                     look

A: Those pants ~~looks~~ cute on you.

B: Really? I no like them very much.

A: Oh, I likes them a lot. And they go well with the shirt. It's a nice outfit. And it doesn't costs much, only $45.

B: Hmm . . . I'm not sure. My brother have a shirt like this. I doesn't want the same thing.

A: What about this shirt? It go well with the pants too.

B: I don't know. It look like my style.

Write about your favorite places to buy clothes.

EXAMPLE: I buy most of my clothes at two stores, O'Neele's and Blackwater River. The clothes are pretty traditional at O'Neele's. They have nice dresses, skirts, and tops. I go to Blackwater River for casual clothes. I buy lots of pants there and shirts and sweaters. Both stores are expensive, so most of the time I only buy things on sale.

_____

_____

_____

_____

Simple Present: *Yes / No* Questions and Short Answers

EXERCISE 1: Simple Present: *Yes / No* Questions

Write the questions in the correct boxes.

1. ~~Do you feel a pain here?~~
2. Do you know how to type?
3. Do you want a plastic bag or a paper bag?
4. Do you have any experience?
5. Do you want a one-bedroom or a two-bedroom apartment?
6. Do you get many headaches?

7. Do you have any fresh fish?
8. Do you speak a foreign language?
9. Do you want a place near the center of town?
10. Does your back hurt?
11. Does this orange juice cost $2.50?
12. Does the house have two bathrooms?

People Often Ask This at . . .

A. a job interview	**B.** a doctor's office *1. Do you feel a pain here?*
C. a real estate office	**D.** a supermarket

EXERCISE 2: Simple Present: *Yes / No* Questions and Short Answers

Match the questions and answers.

<u>e</u> 1. Does the sun go around the Earth?

_____ 2. Do banks have money?

_____ 3. Do you speak English perfectly?

_____ 4. Does Peru have many mountains?

_____ 5. Do supermarkets sell cars?

_____ 6. Does the president of the United States live on the moon?

_____ 7. Does the president of the United States live in the White House?

_____ 8. Do you eat every day?

a. Yes, it does.

b. No, they don't.

c. No, I don't.

d. Yes, I do.

~~e.~~ No, it doesn't.

f. Yes, they do.

g. No, he doesn't.

h. Yes, he does.

EXERCISE 3: Simple Present: *Yes / No* Questions and Short Answers

Answer the questions. Use short answers.

	Michael	Mary	Karen	Larry
Likes rock music	✓	X	X	X
Watches TV every day	X	✓	X	✓
Wakes up early	X	✓	X	✓
Stays up late	X	✓	X	X
Studies at night	✓	X	X	✓

✓ = Yes   X = No

1. Does Michael like rock music? <u>Yes, he does.</u>

2. Do Karen and Larry stay up late? <u>No, they don't.</u>

3. Does Mary wake up early? _____

4. Does Karen study at night? _____

5. Do Michael and Larry study at night? _____

6. Does Mary watch TV every day? _____

7. Do Karen and Michael watch TV every day? _____

8. Does Larry stay up late? _____

9. Do Mary and Larry wake up early? _____

10. Do Karen and Larry like rock music? _____

Complete the sentences. Use **don't** or **doesn't**.

1. Bell Mall has a music store, but Northshore Mall _____*doesn't*_____.

2. I go shopping a lot, but my friends _____*don't*_____.

3. My son wears a tie to work, but my husband _____.

4. Katie has a lot of jewelry, but her sister _____.

5. Ellen and Dave spend a lot of money on clothes, but Bea and Ken _____.

6. My friend buys used clothes, but I _____.

7. Yoko polishes her nails, but her roommates _____.

8. These shoes cost over $100, but the shoes over there _____.

9. My mother likes shopping, but I _____.

10. My classmates and I wear fashionable clothes, but our teacher _____.

Complete the questions.

1. People do not come here on Sundays.

   ___*Do they come*_____ on Saturdays?

2. Carlos has class on Mondays and Wednesdays.

   _____ class on Tuesdays too?

3. The children like bananas.

   _____ apples too?

4. We live in a house.

   _____ in a big house?

5. My boyfriend knows my brother.

   _____ your sister?

6. My wife and I want a hotel room.

   _____ a room for one or two nights?

(continued on next page)

7. I have two sisters.

_____ any brothers?

8. Ms. Winchester doesn't wear glasses.

_____ contact lenses?

9. My classmates and I do not like grammar exercises.

_____ vocabulary exercises?

10. I do not know the answer to the first question.

_____ the answer to the second question?

11. The saleswomen do not work in the afternoon.

_____ in the morning?

12. That young man does not come from the United States.

_____ from Canada?

EXERCISE 6: Editing

Correct the mistake in each sentence.

       Do you
1. ~~You~~ need any help?

2. Does your roommate likes your girlfriend?

3. The teacher wear glasses?

4. Do Mr. Flagg have a car?

5. Does your roommates always sleep late?

6. Peter eat fast?

7. Are she leave for work at the same time every day?

8. Is loud music bother you?

9. Does the doctor has your telephone number?

10. Football players play in the summer?

Imagine you want a room in a dormitory. Write questions to ask the dormitory manager in an email.

EXAMPLE: *Is the dormitory noisy? Do all the rooms have Internet service? Does the room come with a bed?*

1. _____

2. _____

3. _____

4. _____

5. _____

Simple Present: *Wh-* Questions

EXERCISE 1: Question Words

Write the correct question words. Use **who, what, where, when, how,** *or* **why.**

1. _____*What*_____ ?   Cereal.

2. _____*Why*_____ ?   Because I'm tired.

3. _____ ?   At City Central Bank.

4. _____ ?   A suit and tie.

5. _____ ?   My teacher.

6. _____ ?   At noon.

7. _____ ?   His friends.

8. _____ ?   At his school.

9. _____ ?   In the morning.

10. _____ ?   Because I want to buy a new computer.

11. _____ ?   Great.

12. _____ ?   In August.

EXERCISE 2: Simple Present: *Wh-* Questions

Write questions. Then find an answer for each question in Exercise 1. Write the answers below.

1. want / to leave / do / Why / you

   ___*Why do you want to leave*_____ ?   *Because I'm tired.*

2. for breakfast / What / you / have / do

   _____ ?   _____

3. feel / after / do / a nap / How / you

   _____ ?   _____

4. your / corrects / homework / Who

   _____ ?   _____

5. does / work / Rosita / Where

_____? _____

6. on vacation / When / go / you and your family / do

_____? _____

7. What / to work / wear / you / do

_____? _____

8. need / do / more money / you / Why

_____? _____

9. lunch / What time / eat / the kids / do

_____? _____

10. come / the / mail / does / When

_____? _____

11. Doug / soccer / play / Where / does

_____? _____

12. visit / does / on Sundays / Mark / Who

_____? _____

EXERCISE 3: Question Words

Complete the sentences. Use **who, what, where, when, how,** *or* **why.**

ROB: _____Who_____ gets up early?
          1.

NAN: My husband does. He gets up at 4:00 A.M.

ROB: _____ does he get up?
          2.

NAN: He uses an alarm clock.

ROB: _____ does he get up so early?
          3.

NAN: He starts work at 5:30.

ROB: _____ does he do?
          4.

NAN: He's a chef.

ROB: _____ does he work?
          5.

(continued on next page)

NAN: He works downtown. He has his own restaurant.

ROB: _____ does the restaurant open?
  6.

NAN: At seven o'clock.

ROB: Then _____ does he go to work so early?
  7.

NAN: He has to open the door. The other workers come at 5:30 too.

ROB: And _____ do you do in the morning?
  8.

NAN: I sleep.

EXERCISE 4: *Wh-* Questions About the Subject and Object

Complete the questions. Circle the correct answers and write them on the lines.

1. A: What _____*happens*_____ during
   REM sleep?

  (**a.**) happens   **b.** does happen

  B: People sleep deeply.

2. A: Why _____ REM sleep?

  a. need   **b.** do we need

  B: Without it, we can't think clearly.

3. A: Who _____?

  a. dreams   **b.** does dream

  B: Everybody dreams.

4. A: What _____ nightmares?

  a. causes   **b.** do they cause

  B: There are many different causes.

5. A: Who _____ dreams more,
   men or women?

  a. remembers   **b.** do men or women
                             remember

  B: There's no difference between
   men and women.

6. A: What _____ about?

  a. dreams   **b.** do people dream

  B: They dream about many different
   things.

7. A: When _____ to dream?

  a. starts   **b.** do we start

  B: We start at a very young age.

8. A: Why _____ some
   people remember their dreams?

  a. do   **b.** do they

  B: Because they are creative.

Write the questions. Use **who, what, where, when, how,** *or* **why.**

1. _How do you feel after work?_____

   I feel tired.

2. _____

   I drink tea at night because it helps me sleep.

3. _____

   I don't remember a lot about my dream, but it was scary.

4. _____

   In the morning? My roommate looks terrible.

5. _____

   Teenagers sleep late because they need a lot of sleep.

6. _____

   My roommate? She sleeps in the living room.

7. _____

   My mother usually wakes me up, but sometimes my father does.

8. _____

   We sleep late only on the weekends.

9. _____

   In the small bedroom? My little sister sleeps there.

10. _____

    After my nap? I exercise.

11. _____

    In my family? My brother sleeps a lot.

12. _____

    She wakes up very early in the morning.

EXERCISE 6: Editing

Correct the conversation. There are six mistakes. The first mistake is already corrected.
Find and correct five more.

         How often

A: ~~How~~ do you have nightmares?

B: Not very often. Maybe once a year. But unfortunately, my son has nightmares

frequently.

A: What dreams he about?

B: We're not sure. He wakes up crying during the night.

A: Who does go to his room?

B: Sometimes I do. Sometimes my husband does. Or sometimes he runs into our room.

A: What you tell him?

B: Different things.

A: Why does he has nightmares?

B: Because he's afraid of a lot of different things.

A: How he does feel in the morning?

B: He never remembers anything.

EXERCISE 7: Personal Writing

Imagine you are going to help a friend understand his or her dreams. Write down
questions to ask. Use **when, where, what, why, how,** *and* **how often.**

    EXAMPLE: *When do you dream?*

_____

_____

_____

_____

PART IV

THERE IS / THERE ARE; POSSESSIVES; MODALS: ABILITY AND PERMISSION

UNIT 11 There is / There are

EXERCISE 1: *There is* and *There are*: Affirmative Statements

Complete the conversation. Use **there is** *or* **there are***. Remember to add the correct capitalization.*

A: Is anyone in the house?

B: Yes, _____*there are*_____ two men. _____*There is*_____ also a woman. Oh,
           1.   **2.**
_____ two little boys too.
           3.

A: And in the yard?

B: _____ a dog, and _____ three other children.
           4.   **5.**

A: What's in the garage?

B: _____ some boxes.
           6.

A: What's in them?

B: I don't know, but _____ also a motorcycle. _____ two
                              7.   **8.**
cars too.

A: Two?

B: Uh-huh. _____ a TV there too.
                    9.

A: A TV? In the garage? That's strange.

B: And _____ a sofa.
               10.

A: That's really strange!

Put the words in the correct order. Make sentences.

1. stores / the mall / are / in / There

   <u>There are stores in the mall.</u>

2. is / computer / a / There / in / the store

   _____

3. the first floor / There / restaurants / on / are / two

   _____

4. people / There / the door / at / are

   _____

5. amusement park / the mall / is / near / an / There

   _____

6. between / There / the cafés / a / is / bookstore

   _____

7. an / is / There / the second floor / on / international market

   _____

8. are / There / the floor / boxes / on

   _____

9. five / near / There / the man and woman / children / are

   _____

EXERCISE 3: *There is* and *There are*: Affirmative Statements

What's for sale at the yard sale? Write sentences. Use **there is** *or* **there are**.

1. There is a telephone for sale.

2. There are suitcases for sale.

3. _____

4. _____

5. _____

6. _____

7. _____

8. _____

9. _____

10. _____

11. _____

12. _____

13. _____

EXERCISE 4: *There is, There isn't, There are,* and *There aren't*: Affirmative Statements

Write sentences about Vacation Hotel. Use **there is, there isn't, there are,** *or* **there aren't.**

VACATION HOTEL

In every room:
- a bathroom
- two beds
- two closets
- a TV
- an air conditioner

At the hotel:
- two restaurants
- four tennis courts
- two parking lots

1. (a bathroom in every room)   There is a bathroom in every room.

2. (an Internet connection
   in every room)   There isn't an Internet connection in every room.

3. (two beds in every room)   _____

4. (two closets in every room)   _____

5. (a telephone in every room)   _____

6. (a television in every room)   _____

7. (an air conditioner in every room)   _____

8. (a refrigerator in every room)   _____

9. (a swimming pool at the hotel)   _____

10. (two restaurants at the hotel)   _____

11. (four tennis courts at the hotel)   _____

12. (gift shops at the hotel)   _____

13. (two parking lots at the hotel)   _____

Write sentences about the lake area. Use **there are, there aren't, they are,** *or* **they aren't** *and the information below.*

Your Guide to Stores and Services in the Lake Area

Bakeries	2	Not open on Sundays
Department stores	0	
Banks	2	On Main Street
Clothing stores	3	Not very expensive
Bookstores	0	
Drugstores	4	Small
Gas stations	3	In the center of town
Hospitals	0	
Movie theaters	0	
Restaurants	2	Open for lunch and dinner
Schools	3	Not far from Main Street
Supermarkets	2	Big
Indoor swimming pools	0	

1. There are two bakeries. They aren't open on Sundays.

2. There aren't any department stores.

3. _____

4. _____

5. _____

6. _____

(continued on next page)

7. _____

8. _____

9. _____

10. _____

11. _____

12. _____

13. _____

EXERCISE 6: *Are there*: *Yes / No* Questions and Short Answers

Look at the picture. Answer the questions. Use short answers.

1. Are there any stores?   Yes, there are. _____

2. Are there any people?   _____

3. Are there any dogs?   _____

4. Are there any children?   _____

5. Are there any flowers?   _____

6. Are there any restaurants? _____

7. Are there any trees?   _____

8. Are there any police officers? _____

9. Are there any stairs?   _____

Write questions. Then answer them.

1. many elephants in Florida

   <u>Are there many elephants in Florida?</u>   <u>No, there aren't.</u>

2. many elephants in India

   _____   _____

3. a desert in Canada

   _____   _____

4. camels in Saudi Arabia

   _____   _____

5. a long river in the Sahara Desert

   _____   _____

6. many lions in Russia

   _____   _____

7. mountains in Kenya

   _____   _____

8. many people in Antarctica

   _____   _____

9. big city in Thailand

   _____   _____

10. a monkey in your garden

    _____   _____

EXERCISE 8: *There, It, She,* and *They*

Complete the conversation. Use **there, there's, it's, she's, they're,** *or* **there are.**
Remember to add the correct capitalization.

A: Is _____there_____ an office supply store in this mall?
1.

B: Yes, _____ is. _____ next to the
2.   3.

bookstore. Why? What do you want to get?

A: _____ a problem with my computer, so I'm thinking about
4.

getting a new one.

B: Oh, _____ aren't any computers in the office supply
5.

store. But _____ an electronics store in the mall.
6.

_____ on the second floor.
7.

A: Do you mind if we go there?

B: No, let's go. _____ some stairs near here.
8.

_____ near the food court.
9.

[A few minutes later in the electronics store.]

A: So where are the computers?

B: I think _____ in the back of the store, but I'm not sure.
10.

A: _____ a saleswoman. Let's ask her.
11.

B: Where?

A: Over there. _____ wearing a yellow T-shirt.
12.

EXERCISE 9: Editing

Correct the conversation. There are eight mistakes. The first mistake is already corrected. Find and correct seven more.

A: ~~There is~~ *Is there* a food court in the mall?

B: Yes, it is. There is on the second floor. There is eight or ten places with different kinds

of food.

A: Is it a place with Chinese food?

B: I think so. But there isn't any with Japanese food.

A: What about pizza places? Are there any?

B: No, but there are a great pizza place next to the mall. They have all kinds of pizza

and there are delicious.

EXERCISE 10: Personal Writing

Write about an attraction in your town.

EXAMPLE: *There's a wonderful amusement park in my town. It's called Great Woods. There are a lot of exciting rides, and at night there is live music. Sometimes there is rock music, sometimes there is hip-hop, and sometimes there is jazz. You can spend the whole day there. There are different fast-food places, and parking is free. There are two huge parking lots.*

_____

_____

_____

_____

EXERCISE 1: Possessive Nouns

Look at the pictures. Complete the sentences.

1. The wallet is _____ *Al Green's* _____.

2. The handbag is _____.

3. The car is _____.

4. The sweatshirt is _____.

5. The notebook is _____.

6. The jeans are _____.

7. The desk is _____.

8. The composition is _____.

9. The shoes are _____.

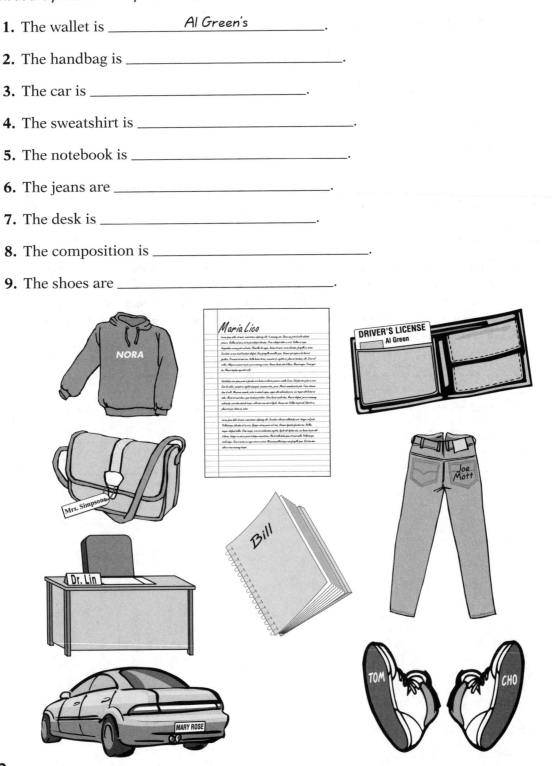

Complete the chart with the correct subject pronouns, object pronouns, possessive adjectives, and possessive pronouns.

Subject Pronoun	Object Pronoun	Possessive Adjective	Possessive Pronoun
I	me	my	mine
		your	
	him		
		her	
it			
			ours
	them		

EXERCISE 3: Possessive Adjectives

Complete the conversations. Use **my, your, his, her, our,** or **their.**

1.   **JACK:** Is that my car?

       JILL: No, _____your_____ car isn't here.

2.   **BOB:** Jim, is this _____ bag?

       JIM: No, it isn't. Maybe it's Sue and Harry's bag.

       BOB: No, _____ bag is over there.

3. **MR. WOLF:** Is this Mrs. Waller's box?

  BARBARA: No, that's not _____ box.

 MR. WOLF: Is it Mr. Luca's box?

  BARBARA: Maybe it's _____ box. I'm not sure.

4.   **MRS. YU:** Is this your family's dog?

      BEN: No, _____ dog is black.

  MRS. YU: Is it Mr. and Mrs. Haley's dog?

      BEN: No, _____ dog is white.

(continued on next page)

5. **ALAN:** Is this your office?

   RON: No, _____ office is on the second floor.

   ALAN: Is it Norma's office?

   RON: No, _____ office is on the first floor.

6. **BECKY:** Stella, is that _____ husband with you in the picture?

   STELLA: Yes, _____ name is Dave.

   BECKY: And who's this?

   STELLA: It's _____ daughter. _____ name is Marie.

EXERCISE 4: Possessive Adjectives and Subject Pronouns

Complete the sentences. Use subject pronouns or possessive adjectives. Remember to add the correct capitalization.

1. Hi. I'm Claudia. ____I____'m from Colombia. ___My___ home is in Bogotá.

2. This is Henry. _____'s from Chicago. _____ apartment is always neat and

   clean.

3. This is Lisa. _____'s from New Jersey. Claudia is _____ roommate.

4. This is Tom, and this is Joanna. _____'re married. _____ last name is Kavalas.

   This is _____ home. _____'s beautiful.

5. Hello. I'm Joe and this is Bill. _____'re friends. _____ homes are in Arizona.

6. Hi. I'm Bruce. _____'m not married, but _____'m engaged. _____ fiancée is

   from Russia.

7. This is Angela Woods. _____'s an accountant. _____ office is on Franklin

   Street.

8. My wife and I are happy to meet you. _____'re here on business. _____ hotel

   is near here. _____ name is the Park Hotel. _____'s a very nice place, but

   _____'s expensive.

9. These are our children. _____ names are Jill and Paul. _____'re not at home

   this month. _____'re with my in-laws.

Rewrite the sentences. Change the underlined words to subject pronouns or possessive adjectives.

1. <u>Mark Gold's</u> an engineer.

   He's an engineer.

2. <u>Mark Gold's</u> wife's a dentist.

   His wife's a dentist.

3. Mariana's <u>Mr. and Mrs. Gold's</u> neighbor.

   _____

4. <u>Mariana's</u> last name is Martinez.

   _____

5. <u>Mariana's</u> an aunt.

   _____

6. Danny and Frederico are <u>Mariana's</u> nephews.

   _____

7. <u>Danny's</u> eight years old.

   _____

8. <u>Frederico's</u> eyes are blue.

   _____

9. <u>Mariana's</u> dogs are always outside.

   _____

10. <u>Danny's</u> afraid of the dogs.

    _____

11. <u>The boys</u> were with their aunt yesterday.

    _____

12. <u>Mariana</u> was with her dogs.

    _____

(continued on next page)

13. The dogs' food was in the garage.

_____

14. The dogs were in the garage.

_____

15. The children's friends were not with them yesterday.

_____

16. The children were happy to be with their aunt.

_____

EXERCISE 6: Possessive Adjectives and Possessive Pronouns

Write **correct** _if the sentence is correct. Write_ **car** _in the sentences where a noun is necessary._

1. Your is not working. _Your car is not working._ _____

2. Mine is not working. _Correct_ _____

3. Is this yours? _____

4. Ours is over there. _____

5. Please bring me my. _____

6. Where is her? _____

7. Give me hers, please. _____

8. Theirs is on Park Street. _____

9. We need our. _____

10. Their is expensive. _____

11. I like mine a lot. _____

12. Why do you want your? _____

EXERCISE 7: Possessive Pronouns

Complete the sentences. Use the correct possessive pronoun. Remember to add the correct capitalization.

1. **A:** Is that her bicycle?

   B: No, _____hers_____ is blue.

2. **A:** Is that your jacket?

   B: No, _____mine_____ is gray.

3. **A:** Is that his classroom?

   B: No, _____ is on the fifth floor.

4. **A:** Is that our suitcase?

   B: No, _____ is not light brown. We have a dark brown suitcase.

5. These are not your shoes. _____ are under the bed.

6. **A:** Is that their house?

   B: No, _____ is on Middle Street.

7. **A:** Are those your son's sneakers?

   B: No, _____ are a size 12.

8. **A:** Is that Ms. Gilman's office?

   B: No, _____ is in the next building.

9. These are not Yuri's and Natasha's test papers. _____ are on my desk.

10. My roommate and I have a sofa like that one, but _____ is a little bigger.

EXERCISE 8: Possessive Adjectives and Possessive Pronouns

Complete the conversations. Use the correct possessive adjective or possessive pronoun. Remember to add the correct capitalization.

1. **A:** This is not _____my_____ coat.

   B: Where's _____yours_____?

   A: In the closet.

2. **A:** That's _____ ball. Give it to me!

   B: It's not _____. It's _____. It's a birthday present from my

   brother.

(continued on next page)

3. **A:** Whose scarf is this?

   B: It's Nancy's.

   A: Are you sure it's _____? This scarf is green, and she rarely wears green.

   B: I'm sure it's _____.

4. **A:** We're so happy with _____ new car. We love it.

   B: You're lucky. We don't like _____ at all.

5. **A:** Do you know Bonnie and Tony Garcia? _____ son is on the football team.

   B: We know them, but we don't know _____ son. Our son is on the middle school team, but _____ is on the high school team.

6. **A:** Is this your husband's hat?

   B: Yes, it is.

   A: How do you know it's _____?

   B: Because all of _____ hats have his name inside.

EXERCISE 9: Questions with *Whose*

Larry is at the supermarket. He has the wrong bag of food. Write questions. Use **whose**.

1. This is not my coffee.

   Whose coffee is this?

2. These are not my apples.

   Whose apples are these?

3. These are not my eggs.

   _____

4. These are not my bananas.

   _____

5. This is not my bread.

   _____

6. These are not my potatoes.

   _____

7. This is not my cake.

   _____

8. This is not my milk.

   _____

9. This is not my orange juice.

   _____

10. These are not my potato chips.

    _____

11. These are not my carrots.

    _____

12. This is not my bag.

    _____

EXERCISE 10: Subject and Object Pronouns

Put the words in the correct order. Write sentences. Remember to add the correct punctuation and capitalization.

1. love / you / I   I love you. _____

2. him / she / loves   _____

3. us / love / they   _____

4. we / them / love   _____

5. know / I / you   _____

6. her / you / don't know   _____

EXERCISE 11: Object Pronouns

Complete the sentences. Use the correct object pronoun.

1. **A:** Is this for Mr. Fuentes?

   B: Yes, it's for _____ him _____.

2. **A:** Is this for you and your wife?

   B: Yes, it's for _____.

3. **A:** Is this for your brother and sister?

   B: Yes, it's for _____.

4. **A:** Is this for me?

   B: Yes, it's for _____.

5. **A:** Is this for Maria?

   B: Yes, it's for _____.

6. **A:** Is this for Chris and me?

   B: Yes, it's for _____.

7. **A:** Is this for Ms. Dong?

   B: Yes, it's for _____.

8. **A:** Is this for my neighbors?

   B: Yes, it's for _____.

9. **A:** Is this for you and Ari?

   B: Yes, it's for _____.

10. **A:** Is this for Anna's boyfriend?

    B: Yes, it's for _____.

11. **A:** Is this for the horses?

    B: Yes, it's for _____.

12. **A:** Is this for John?

    B: Yes, it's for _____.

EXERCISE 12: Subject and Object Pronouns

Complete the sentences. Use the correct subject pronoun or object pronoun. Remember to add the correct capitalization.

1. **A:** Is your name Sasha?

   B: Yes, _____*it*_____ is.

2. **A:** This DVD is for you. _____'s for your birthday.

   B: Oh, thank you. I love _____.

3. **A:** Is Maryann your aunt?

   B: Yes, _____ is.

   A: Please give _____ this package.

4. **A:** My brother is over there.

   B: I like _____. _____ is handsome.

5. **A:** Are you busy?

   B: Yes, _____ am. Please call _____ later.

6. **A:** Here are two dishes.

   B: But _____'re dirty. Please wash _____.

7. **A:** Are you and Lee free on Sunday?

   B: Yes, _____ are. Visit _____ then.

8. **A:** Hello?

   B: Hello. Is Judi there?

   A: Yes. Just a minute. Judi! Judi! This call is for _____.

EXERCISE 13: Review of Pronouns and Possessives

Complete the sentences. Choose the correct words in parentheses. (Use only three of the words.) Remember to add the correct capitalization.

1. **(I, me, mine, my)**

   The laptop is _____*mine*_____. _____*My*_____ parents bought it for

   _____*me*_____ last year.

2. (our, ours, us, we)

Hello. _____ last name is Todd. _____ called an hour ago.

Do you have a table for _____?

3. (our, ours, us, we)

Excuse me. _____ don't want to bother you, but those seats are

_____. Here are _____ tickets.

4. (I, me, my, mine)

Please introduce _____ to the man at the table. He's _____

neighbor, but _____ don't know him.

5. (he, him, his, his)

That hat belongs to my brother. _____ name is in it. The jacket is

_____ too. Please give the hat and jacket to _____.

6. (you, you, your, yours)

Those aren't _____ keys. _____ are on the table.

_____ always forget something.

7. (it, it, it's, its)

I rarely read that magazine. _____ is hard to find in my neighborhood,

and I don't like _____ very much. _____ articles are often

long and boring.

8. (their, theirs, them, they)

The car is _____ father's. It isn't _____. He often gives the

car to _____ on the weekend.

9. (her, her, hers, she)

Do you know _____? _____ is my neighbor. The dog is

_____.

EXERCISE 14: Editing

Correct the conversations. There are ten mistakes. The first mistake is already corrected. Find and correct nine more.

1. **A:** Is this Steve͜ᐱcomposition? ᐟs

   B: I don't think so.

2. **A:** What's Ms. Baker first name?

   B: It's Sandra.

3. **A:** Where's the men room?

   B: It's over there. Do you see its?

4. **A:** Whose handwriting is this?

   B: It's my.

5. **A:** Are your brothers wives friendly?

   B: Yes, I like her very much.

6. **A:** Who's books are these? Are they yours or Miriam's?

   B: They're hers.

7. **A:** I can't find my teacher.

   B: Look in the teachers lunchroom. Many teachers are in there.

8. **A:** Where are Elena and Sam?

   B: They're not here, but theirs bags are in the back of the room.

EXERCISE 15: Personal Writing

Write about your best friend. Use pronouns and possessive adjectives.

EXAMPLE: My best friend's name is Tom. He's from Toronto, and he is crazy about basketball. He doesn't play it, but he goes to all the Toronto Raptors' games. That's his favorite team, and he really loves the players. He has pictures of them all over his bedroom wall, and he knows all their names, all 18 of them.

_____

_____

_____

_____

EXERCISE 1: Ability

Look at the job advertisements. Look at the qualifications of Martha, Frank, Les, and Rosa. Then answer the questions.

WANTED
SECRETARY
CENTRAL ANIMAL HOSPITAL
Good typing and computer skills
Need to speak Spanish

FARM WORKER WANTED
Must be able to control animals
Use heavy equipment
Work long days

WANTED
DRIVER FOR PET FOOD COMPANY
Drive truck
Pick up boxes and deliver to pet stores

WANTED
DOG WALKER
Manage 6–10 dogs
Walk for long distances

	MARTHA	FRANK	LES	ROSA
Manage dogs	no	no	yes	yes
Drive	no	yes	yes	no
Lift 100 pounds	no	no	yes	no
Walk long distances	yes	no	no	yes
Control animals	no	yes	no	yes
Speak Spanish	yes	no	no	yes
Work long days	yes	yes	no	yes
Type	yes	yes	no	no
Use heavy equipment	no	yes	no	no

1. Which job is good for Rosa? The job as a _____ *dog walker* _____.

2. Which job is good for Frank? The job as a _____.

3. Which job is good for Les? The job as a _____.

4. Which job is good for Martha? The job as a _____.

EXERCISE 2: *Can* for Ability: Affirmative and Negative Statements

Look at the information in Exercise 1 again. Then answer the questions. Use **can** *or* **can't.**

1. Why is the job as dog walker good for Rosa?

   She _can manage dogs and walk long distances._

2. Why isn't the job as dog walker good for Martha?

   She _can walk long distances, but she can't manage dogs._

3. Why isn't the job as dog walker good for Frank?

   He _can't manage dogs, and he can't walk long distances._

4. Why is the job as driver good for Les?

   He _____

5. Why is the job as secretary good for Martha?

   She _____

6. Why is the job as farm worker good for Frank?

   He _____

7. Why isn't the job as secretary good for Les?

   He _____

8. Why isn't the job as driver good for Martha?

   She _____

9. Why isn't the job as farm worker good for Rosa?

   She _____

10. Why isn't the job as dog walker good for Les?

    He _____

11. Why isn't the job as driver good for Frank?

    She _____

12. Why isn't the job as secretary good for Rosa?

    She _____

Write questions. Use **can.** *Then answer the questions, using short answers.*

1. you / drive

    Can you drive?   *Yes, I can.* OR *No, I can't.*

2. your mother / lift 100 pounds

_____   _____

3. your father / play the guitar

_____   _____

4. your best friend / ride a horse

_____   _____

5. your parents / speak Spanish

_____   _____

6. you / swim

_____   _____

7. you / type

_____   _____

8. your parakeet / talk

_____   _____

9. your dog / do tricks

_____   _____

10. your cat / catch mice

_____   _____

Complete the sentences. Use **could** *or* **couldn't** *and the verbs in parentheses.*

1. I'm sorry that I _____*couldn't call*_____ you yesterday. I was very busy.
   (call)

2. We enjoyed our holiday in Spain because we _____ our
   (practice)
   Spanish.

3. We _____ to the party last night. Our son was sick.
   (go)

4. The test was really hard. I _____ all the questions.
   (answer)

5. I had a bad stomachache yesterday. I _____ a thing.
   (eat)

6. The work in high school was easy. I _____ soccer every
   (play)
   weekend.

7. The movie was sold out. We _____ any tickets.
   (get)

8. Our hotel room wasn't good. We _____ the people in the other
   (hear)
   rooms.

9. It wasn't warm on the weekend. We _____ swimming.
   (go)

10. My summer vacation was great. I _____ whatever I wanted.
    (do)

EXERCISE 5: Editing

Correct this conversation. There are six mistakes. The first mistake is already corrected.
Find and correct five more.

A: So how was dog training class? Can Charlie ~~to do~~ *do* any new tricks?

B: Nope. He's just not as intelligent as the other dogs. They can doing lots of tricks but

Charlie can't.

A: Like what?

B: Well, he no can roll over. All of the other dogs could did that in yesterday's class, but

not Charlie.

A: What else the other dogs can do?

B: They can get the newspaper and bring it back.

A: That's strange. Charlie can do that last week. He did it for me.

Write about a pet you or someone you know had many years ago. Use **could** *or* **couldn't.**

EXAMPLE: *Until 2006 my friend Warren had a dog named Heidi. Heidi died when she was nine years old. She was a very smart dog. She could always find me when I was lost. She could swim too. She couldn't talk, but she could always understand me. Warren said she could catch fish, but I never saw her do that!*

_____

_____

_____

_____

EXERCISE 1: *Can* or *May* in Statements

Complete the sentences. Circle the correct answers and write them on the lines.

1. The doctor says, "You ___can___ call me at night. It's not a problem."

   a. can

   b. can't

2. The teacher says, "You _____ use your cell phone in class. Do not bring your phone to class."

   a. can

   b. can't

3. Sam's father says, "You _____ drive my car. You're too young."

   a. may

   b. may not

4. The police officer says, "You _____ park in front of a bus stop. Move your car."

   a. can

   b. can't

5. The nurse says, "You _____ go into the room now. Dorothy is waiting for you."

   a. may

   b. may not

6. The store manager says, "You _____ smoke in the store. It's against the law."

   a. can

   b. can't

7. Karen's mother says, "You _____ go to the movies, but be home before eleven o'clock."

   a. can

   b. can't

8. The office manager says, "You _____ leave at four o'clock, but not before then."

    a. may

    b. may not

9. The doctor says, "You _____ gain more weight. It's bad for your health."

    a. can

    b. can't

EXERCISE 2: *May* and *Can* for Polite Requests

Complete the requests. Use the words from the box.

bring my boyfriend	~~open the window~~	sit here
come in	pay by credit card	speak to the doctor

1. A: I'm cold. May I _open the window_ ?

    B: Yes, you may.

2. A: The total is $109.50.

    B: Can I _____ ?

    A: Sure.

3. A: Mark, is that you at the door?

    B: Yes, it is. May I _____ ?

    A: Of course.

4. A: Hello. Dr. Asbury's office. Connie speaking.

    B: Hello. This is Chris Nelson. Can I _____ ?

    A: I'm sorry, but he's with a patient.

5. A: Hello.

    B: Hello. May I _____ ?

    A: Sure. The seat's free.

6. A: Please come to my party next Saturday.

    B: Can I _____ ?

    A: Of course.

Make polite requests. Use **may I** *or* **can I.**

1. You have a doctor's appointment at four o'clock. You want to leave early because class ends at four o'clock. Ask your teacher.

   Can I leave class early? OR *May I leave class early?*

2. You're in a friend's room. You're hot and you want to open the window. Ask your friend.

   _____

3. You're in an office. You want to use the telephone on the secretary's desk. Ask the secretary.

   _____

4. Your classmate has a car, but you don't have one. It's raining, and you want to get a ride. Ask your classmate.

   _____

5. You made a mistake. You don't have an eraser, but your classmate has an eraser. Ask your classmate.

   _____

6. You're at your neighbor's house. You want to have a drink of water. Ask your neighbor.

   _____

7. You have a question about something in your grammar book. Ask your teacher.

   _____

8. You're at a restaurant. You want to sit at the empty table in the corner. Ask the waiter.

   _____

EXERCISE 4: Editing

Correct the conversation. There are six mistakes. The first mistake is already corrected.
Find and correct five more.

RECEPTIONIST: Can I ~~may~~ help you?

BOB: May I seeing the nurse? I don't feel well.

RECEPTIONIST: Yes, may you go in. The nurse's office is the first door on the right.

[15 minutes later.]

NURSE: Here, take this medicine twice a day.

BOB: May I takes some now?

NURSE: No, wait until dinnertime.

BOB: When I can go back to class? May I to go tomorrow?

NURSE: No, wait until next week. You can go back to class then.

EXERCISE 5: Personal Writing

*Write about what people in your family can and can't do at dinner. Use **can, can't, may**,*
*or **may not**.*

EXAMPLE: *At my house we can invite friends to dinner. We can also bring food from outside.*
We can't come late to dinner. At the table we can talk about our day or about
politics, but we can't interrupt each other. Also, we can't have fights. We may not
read at the table or put our elbows on the table. And we may not talk with food
in our mouth.

_____

_____

_____

_____

UNIT 15 Present Progressive: Affirmative and Negative Statements

EXERCISE 1: Present Progresive: Affirmative Statements

What are the people doing? Match the sentences.

_d_ 1. Jane is in math class.

____ 2. Paul's at the ATM.

____ 3. Linda's in the library.

____ 4. The players are on the field.

____ 5. Doug's at the shopping mall.

____ 6. Dr. Miller is in her office.

____ 7. Susan's in the bathroom.

____ 8. Ms. Thompson and her family are in the dining room.

____ 9. Sharon and her boyfriend are at the beach.

____ 10. Pete's at the office.

a. They're playing football.

b. She's studying.

c. She's examining a patient.

d. She's taking a test.

e. He's getting some money.

f. They're eating dinner.

g. She's taking a shower.

h. They're lying in the sun.

i. He's writing a report.

j. He's buying a shirt.

EXERCISE 2: Base Form of Verb + -ing

Write the missing form of each verb.

Base Form	Base Form + -ing
1. have	*having*
2. *sit*	sitting
3. smile	_____
4. shine	_____
5. _____	raining
6. _____	making

Base Form	Base Form + -ing
7. sleep	_____
8. listen	_____
9. _____	running
10. hold	_____
11. _____	talking
12. hope	_____
13. do	_____
14. _____	putting
15. _____	beginning
16. read	_____
17. _____	crying
18. stay	_____

EXERCISE 3: Present Progressive Statements with *Right now* and *These days*

Write **right now** *or* **these days** *about each sentence.*

1. Prices are going up.   <u>these days</u>

2. He's talking to the teacher.   <u>right now</u>

3. I'm getting you some water.   _____

4. We're getting in the car.   _____

5. Smart phones are getting popular.   _____

6. My girlfriend and I are fighting a lot.   _____

7. The business is not making a lot of money.   _____

8. I'm waking up early.   _____

9. I'm studying. Please be quiet.   _____

10. The students are not learning much.   _____

EXERCISE 4: Present Progressive: Affirmative and Negative Statements

Write affirmative and negative sentences about each picture. Use the present progressive of the verb in parentheses.

1. (sleep) Marcus and Julius _____ *aren't sleeping* _____.

   (play) They _____ *are playing* _____.

2. (stand) Mr. and Mrs. Bell _____ in the Ferris wheel.

   (sit) They _____ in the Ferris wheel.

3. (watch) Sue _____ TV.

   (read) Ted _____ a newspaper.

4. (read) Yukiko and Hiro _____ about Japan.

   (read) They _____ about Mexico.

5. (run) Luis _____.

   (stand) He _____.

6. (hold) Berta _____ a camera
phone.

(talk) She _____ on the phone.

7. (buy) Yumi _____ food from a
vending machine.

(buy) She _____ food at a
supermarket.

8. (smile) Roberto and Marco _____.

(cry) They _____.

EXERCISE 5: Present Progressive: Affirmative and Negative Statements

Write true sentences.

1. I / do / a grammar exercise

   I am doing a grammar exercise. _____

2. I / sleep

   I am not sleeping. _____

3. I / have / a good time

   _____

4. The sun / shine

   _____

5. It / rain

   _____

(continued on next page)

6. It / get / dark

_____

7. I / listen / to the radio

_____

8. I / talk / on the phone

_____

9. I / sit / on a chair

_____

10. My neighbors / make / a lot of noise

_____

EXERCISE 6: Present Progressive: Subject / Verb Agreement

Complete the postcard. Use the correct form of the verbs in parentheses.

January 11

     Greetings from Vermont from all of us. We are
_____ having _____ a great class trip. It
    1. (have)
_____ a little right now, and it
    2. (snow)
is cold. Many people _____ , but
                3. (ski)
we are too tired. We _____ at
             4. (relax)
the moment. Ellen and I _____ in
           5. (sit)
the coffee shop. She _____ , and
       6. (read)
I _____ to you! Mike and Jan
   7. (write)
_____ a snowman outside. They
   8. (make)
_____ themselves a lot. Naturally,
   9. (enjoy)
Tommy _____ a video game!
      10. (play)
   We hope you are well.

           Regards from all of us,

           Nick

To:

   Tom Gerardi
   321 Maple Drive
   Glen Oaks, NJ 02445

Correct the email. There are eight mistakes. The first mistake is already corrected. Find and correct seven more.

Subject: Hi
From: dhidalgo
Date: 09/15/12
To: elsie

Hi,

How are you doing?

                                    I'm not

I'm in between classes right now, so ~~I no am~~ doing anything. I'm sit in the school cafeteria. All the other people around me is eating, but I'm not hungry. I just having a cup of coffee and thinking about my classes.

I'm take some good classes this semester. We doing lots of interesting things, but the classes are tough. Also, there's no time for extra-curricular activities. I'm not get good grades, so I'm a little worried, especially about my math class. But my classmates and I studying hard for our next math test. We study together every Tuesday and Thursday, and it's helping me a lot.

Anyway, that's the news from here.

Danny

EXERCISE 8: Personal Writing

What are you doing right now? Write answers to these questions. Use the present progressive.

> What time is it?
>
> Where are you?
>
> What are you doing?
>
> What are you thinking about?
>
> Is anyone with you? If so, what is that person doing?

EXAMPLE: *It's eight o'clock in the evening, and I'm sitting at the kitchen table. I'm not eating. I'm doing my homework, and I'm listening to the radio. I'm thinking about what to write here, but I'm also thinking about my weekend plans. Nobody is at home with me. My brother is at soccer practice. I don't know where my parents are. Maybe they're visiting my grandparents.*

_____

_____

_____

_____

_____

EXERCISE 1: Present Progressive: *Yes / No* Questions and Answers

*Put the words in the correct order. Write questions. Then write short answers. If you don't know an answer, write **I don't know**.*

1. doing / you / a grammar exercise / Are

   Are you doing a grammar exercise? _____   Yes, I am. _____

2. glasses / wearing / you / Are

   _____   _____

3. your English teacher / correcting / Is / papers

   _____   _____

4. a movie / you and a friend / watching / Are

   _____   _____

5. your classmates / doing / this exercise / now / Are

   _____   _____

6. Are / having / with your neighbors / dinner / you

   _____   _____

7. shining / the sun / Is

   _____   _____

8. your friends / Are / for you / waiting

   _____   _____

9. working / Are / your parents

   _____   _____

10. coughing / Are / you

    _____   _____

(continued on next page)

11. Is / helping / your teacher / you

_____   _____

12. outside / the children / Are / playing

_____   _____

EXERCISE 2: Present Progressive: *Wh-* Questions and Answers

Look at the picture. Read the answers. Then complete the questions with **who, what, where, when,** _or_ **why.**

1. _____*What*_____ is the little girl holding?   A box of markers.

2. _____ is sleeping?   The man.

3. _____ is the man sleeping?   He's tired.

4. _____ is the little girl standing?   Near the man.

5. _____ are the boys watching?   A basketball game.

6. _____ are the boys sitting?   On the sofa.

7. _____ is doing something wrong?   The little girl.

Write questions. Use the words in parentheses.

1. A: Yoko's in class.

    B: _____ *Is she listening to the teacher?* _____ (listen to the teacher)

    A: Probably.

2. A: Mary's in the bedroom.

    B: _____ (sleep)

    A: Maybe.

3. A: All the children are at the playground.

    B: _____ (play)

    A: Probably.

4. A: My son and his friend are at the swimming pool.

    B: _____ (swim)

    A: I think so.

5. A: John's at the ATM machine.

    B: _____ (get money)

    A: Probably.

6. A: My parents are on vacation.

    B: _____ (have a good time)

    A: I hope so.

7. A: Carol's at the hospital.

    B: _____ (visit someone)

    A: I don't know.

8. A: Warren and Anne are outside.

    B: _____ (play tennis)

    A: I think so.

(continued on next page)

9. A: Julie's under the car.

   B: _____ (fix something)

   A: Maybe.

10. A: Michael isn't here yet.

   B: _____ (come)

   A: I think so.

11. A: There are two people in the hall.

   B: _____ (wait for me)

   A: I don't know.

12. A: A man's behind you.

   B: _____ (follow me)

   A: I don't know.

EXERCISE 4: Present Progressive: *Wh-* Questions and Answers

Put the words in the correct order. Write questions.

1. doing / you and Kevin / What / are

   What are you and Kevin doing?

2. watching / are / Why / you / an old movie

   _____

3. the people / are / talking about / What

   _____

4. Who / Kevin / is / meeting

   _____

5. meeting / they / are / Where

   _____

6. are / Why / meeting / they / at the mall

   _____

7. laughing / is / Who

   _____

8. they / What / laughing about / are

_____

9. sitting / you / Where / are

_____

10. are / you / What / eating

_____

EXERCISE 5: Present Progressive: *Wh-* Questions

Write the correct questions from Exercise 4.

1. _Why are you watching an old movie?_____

Because it's one of my favorite movies.

2. _____

His old friends Peter Sanchez and Tommy Maguire.

3. _____

I am watching an old movie. Kevin is meeting some people.

4. _____

Ice cream.

5. _____

Old movies.

6. _____

Tommy works there.

7. _____

Something funny in a movie.

8. _____

In the living room.

9. _____

The actors in the movie.

10. _____

At the mall.

Complete the conversations. Circle the correct answers and write them on the lines.

1. **A:** What are you doing?

   B: I'm talking on the phone.

   A: Who _____*are you talking*_____ to?

       a. is talking   **(b.)** are you talking

   B: A friend.

2. **A:** What are you doing?

   B: I'm cooking for the party.

   A: Who _____ to the party?

       a. is coming   **b.** are they coming

   B: Some people from work.

3. **A:** Where's Conor?

   B: He's playing in the backyard.

   A: Who _____ with?

       a. is playing   **b.** is he playing

   B: Some friends from school.

4. **A:** The music is nice.

   B: Yes, it is.

   A: Who _____?

       a. is playing   **b.** is he playing

   B: My son.

5. **A:** What are you doing?

   B: I'm writing a letter.

   A: Who _____?

       a. is writing   **b.** are you writing to

   B: My cousin.

6. A: Are the kids at home?

   B: No, they're helping someone with some packages.

   A: Who _____?

      a. is helping   **b.** are they helping

   B: The older couple down the street.

7. A: Nurse Richards, is anybody still waiting in the office?

   B: Yes.

   A: Who _____?

      a. is waiting   **b.** are they waiting

   B: Ms. Gomez and Mr. Robertson.

EXERCISE 7: Present Progressive: *Wh-* Questions

Write questions. Use the present progressive.

1. A: Doug is painting something.

   B: *What is he painting?* _____

   A: I'm not sure. I think it's a portrait.

2. A: I'm reading.

   B: _____

   A: A very good book.

3. A: The kids are coughing.

   B: _____

   A: They're catching a cold.

4. A: My husband's cooking.

   B: _____

   A: Dinner.

5. A: Someone's coming.

   B: _____

   A: I think it's your sister.

(continued on next page)

6. A: I'm going to bed.

B: _____

A: I'm tired.

7. A: We're going.

B: _____

A: To the supermarket.

8. A: I'm selling my car.

B: _____

A: It's old.

9. A: Monica and Chris are swimming.

B: _____

A: In the pool near the park.

10. A: I'm watching TV.

B: _____

A: The baseball game.

11. A: The police officers are watching someone.

B: _____

A: That young man over there.

12. A: Jane's dating someone new.

B: _____

A: Eric Snyder.

EXERCISE 8: Editing

Correct the conversation. There are six mistakes. The first mistake is already corrected.
Find and correct five more.

A: Are you ~~watch~~ *watching* the game?

B: No, I'm watching an old movie. This is one of my favorite scenes.

A: What happening? Who the people are waiting for?

B: They're all standing around and waiting for the wizard.

A: Who's standing in the middle? Is she the wizard?

B: No, she is waiting for the wizard. She needs his help. Look, here he comes now.

A: What he wearing? He is wearing pajamas?

B: No, he's not wearing. Those are his special clothes. They give him special powers.

A: This is a stupid movie. Can we change the channel and watch the game?

EXERCISE 9: Personal Writing

Imagine a friend is watching a movie on TV. You want to know what is happening. Write down questions to ask your friend.

EXAMPLE: What are you watching?
          Who are the actors?

_____

_____

_____

_____

EXERCISE 1: Simple Present

Match the occupations with the activities.

__i__	**1.** artists	**a.** bake bread and cake
____	**2.** bakers	**b.** count money
____	**3.** bank tellers	**c.** cut meat
____	**4.** bus drivers	**d.** do experiments
____	**5.** butchers	**e.** drive buses
____	**6.** doctors	**f.** examine patients
____	**7.** gardeners	**g.** feed animals
____	**8.** mechanics	**h.** fix cars
____	**9.** journalists	**i.** paint pictures
____	**10.** scientists	**j.** serve food
____	**11.** waitresses	**k.** water plants and flowers
____	**12.** zookeepers	**l.** write articles

EXERCISE 2: Simple Present and Present Progressive

Complete the sentences. Use the correct form of the verbs in Exercise 1.

1. Scott's a doctor. He _____ *examines patients* _____ every day. Right now he's

in his office. He _____ *is examining* _____ a patient.

2. Marilyn's a bus driver. She _____ five days a week.

Right now she's at work. She _____ a bus.

3. Larry's a mechanic. Every day he _____. Right now

he's at his garage. He _____ a car.

4. Anne's a waitress. Every day she _____. Right now

she's at the restaurant. She _____ food.

5. Sandra and Peter are artists. They _____

almost every day. Right now they're both at their studios. They

_____ pictures.

6. Nicholas and Catherine are scientists. They _____ every day. Right now they're in the lab. They _____ an experiment.

7. Renée and Cathy are journalists. They _____ every afternoon. They're at work right now. They _____ an article.

8. Arthur's a butcher. He _____ every day. Right now he's at his store. He _____ meat.

9. Linda's a bank teller. She _____ all day long. Right now she's at the bank. She _____ money.

10. Barry and Fred are bakers. They _____ every morning. They're in the kitchen now. They _____ bread and cake.

11. Ruth's a gardener. She _____ almost every day. Right now she's at work. She _____ plants and flowers.

12. Jeffrey's a zookeeper. He _____ two times a day. Right now he's in the elephant house. He _____ the animals.

EXERCISE 3: Action Verbs and Non-Action Verbs

Underline the verb in each sentence. Then write **action verb** *or* **non-action verb.**

1. I <u>love</u> to travel.   _____*non-action verb*_____

2. Does it <u>rain</u> a lot in San Francisco?   _____*action verb*_____

3. All the hotels have swimming pools.   _____

4. Hotel guests have meals in their rooms.   _____

5. We don't know much about the place.   _____

6. Why are you packing the suitcases now?   _____

7. You need a passport.   _____

(continued on next page)

8. I'm writing a postcard to my parents. _____

9. Steve flies to California every month. _____

10. Do you send emails home every day? _____

11. The food looks good. _____

12. He looks at the guidebook constantly. _____

13. Do we owe any money? _____

14. Many tourists visit Paris every year. _____

15. Cell phones are useful on trips. _____

EXERCISE 4: Simple Present and Present Progressive

Complete the sentences. Circle the correct answers and write them on the lines.

1. This phone _____ has _____ a lot of cool features. Here, look.

    (a.) has   **b.** 's having

2. We _____ help. Let's ask the teacher.

    a. need   **b.** 're needing

3. I'm busy. I _____ on the phone.

    a. talk   **b.** 'm talking

4. She _____ it. Explain it to her again.

    a. doesn't understand   **b.** isn't understanding

5. Pedro _____ his family. That's why he's sad.

    a. misses   **b.** 's missing

6. You _____ in the right place. Look over there!

    a. don't look   **b.** aren't looking

7. There's a problem, but I _____ the answer.

    a. don't know   **b.** 'm not knowing

8. I _____. Don't talk to me!

    a. think   **b.** 'm thinking

9. That shirt _____ good. Buy it!

    a. looks   **b.** 's looking

10. _____ that guy is nice?

    a. Do you think   **b.** Are you thinking

11. There's a red cell phone on the table. _____ to you?

    a. Does it belong   **b.** Is it belonging

12. The little boy is unhappy. That's why he _____.

    a. cries   **b.** 's crying

13. Let's stay. I _____ a good time.

    a. have   **b.** 'm having

14. That music _____ terrible. Turn it off!

    a. sounds   **b.** 's sounding

EXERCISE 5: Simple Present and Present Progressive

Complete the conversation. Write the correct form of the verbs in parentheses. Use contractions if possible.

A: What _____ do you want _____ to do now?
          1. (you / want)

B: I _____. _____ to go to the movies?
       2. (not care)   **3. (you / want)**

A: What _____?
       4. (play)

B: I _____. I _____ my phone with me to
      5. (not know)   **6. (not have)**
check online.

A: Well, let's take a walk to the movie theater and see. It's only two blocks away.

B: But it _____.
      7. (rain)

A: So what? I _____ an umbrella.
       8. (have)

B: But I _____ one.
      9. (not have)

A: Well, take mine. I _____ it. This coat
        10. (not need)
_____ waterproof and I _____ the rain.
  11. (be)   **12. (like)**

B: OK. Thanks.

A: Maybe Alex _____ to come with us.
       13. (want)

B: I _____ so. He _____ a lot of homework
   14. (not think)   **15. (have)**
tonight. He _____ it right now.
      16. (do)

(continued on next page)

A: But I _____ his voice. He _____ on
       _{17. (hear)}   _{18. (talk)}

the phone.

B: He _____ to a classmate. There's something he
       _{19. (talk)}

_____, and he _____ some help.
_{20. (not understand)}   _{21. (get)}

A: How _____?
       _{22. (you / know)}

B: I _____ everything.
       _{23. (know)}

A: Well, you _____ what's playing at the movies. So let's go
       _{24. (not know)}

and see!

EXERCISE 6: Editing

Correct the conversation. There are nine mistakes. The first mistake is already corrected. Find and correct eight more.

                                         are you doing

ALAN: Hi, Marsha. This is Alan. What ~~do you do~~ right now?

MARSHA: Oh, hi, Alan. I cut some vegetables for dinner.

ALAN: Are you preparing dinner at this time every evening?

MARSHA: Yeah, usually. We are eating dinner at around 8:00 or 8:30. Why? When do you

have dinner?

ALAN: Oh, my family and I are eating much earlier. The kids are being usually hungry

by 6:30 or 7:00.

MARSHA: Really? Our kids are having a snack at 5:00. Then they're not hungry until 8:00.

So, what's up?

ALAN: Listen. I work on a report for the office, and there is a problem. Are you having

a couple of minutes to talk about it?

MARSHA: Sure.

Write about something you are doing differently these days. Say what you usually do and how things are different now. Use the simple present and present progressive.

EXAMPLE: *I'm living away from home for the first time in my life. I usually live with my family, but right now I'm attending college and living in a dormitory. At home my mother cleans and does my laundry, but here I clean my own room and do my own laundry. It's not a lot of fun. I miss my mother—but not only because I hate to clean!*

_____

_____

_____

_____

UNIT 18 Simple Past: Affirmative and Negative Statements with Regular Verbs

EXERCISE 1: Simple Past: Affirmative and Negative Statements with Regular Verbs

Match the sentences.

_d_ **1.** Sylvia is tired.

____ **2.** Sylvia's worried about her French test.

____ **3.** Sylvia's car is clean.

____ **4.** Sylvia is hungry.

____ **5.** Sylvia is angry.

____ **6.** Sylvia is happy.

____ **7.** Sylvia's talking about a TV program.

____ **8.** Sylvia's grandparents are unhappy.

____ **9.** There's a lot of food in Sylvia's refrigerator.

a. She washed it yesterday.

b. Her boyfriend called her yesterday to say, "I love you."

c. She watched it last night.

d. She didn't sleep much last night.

e. She didn't eat breakfast or lunch.

f. She didn't visit them last weekend.

g. Her boyfriend forgot her birthday.

h. She cooked all day yesterday.

i. She didn't study very much.

EXERCISE 2: Past-Time Markers

Complete the sentences. Use **yesterday** *or* **last.**

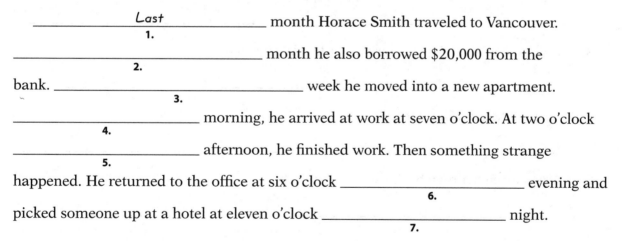

Detective's Notes on Mr. Horace Smith

April 15th Traveled to Vancouver

April 25th Borrowed $20,000

May 13th Moved into new apartment

(Nothing unusual until May 19th)

May 19th
7:00 A.M.   Arrived at work
2:00 P.M.   Finished work
6:00 P.M.   Returned to the office
11:00 P.M. Picked someone up at a hotel

It's Thursday, May 20th. Here's our report on Horace Smith.

_____Last_____ month Horace Smith traveled to Vancouver.
        1.

_____ month he also borrowed $20,000 from the
      2.

bank. _____ week he moved into a new apartment.
        3.

_____ morning, he arrived at work at seven o'clock. At two o'clock
     4.

_____ afternoon, he finished work. Then something strange
     5.

happened. He returned to the office at six o'clock _____ evening and
                                         6.

picked someone up at a hotel at eleven o'clock _____ night.
                                         7.

EXERCISE 3: Simple Past and *Ago*

A. *Answer the questions.*

    a. What day of the week is it today? _____

    b. What month is it now?   _____

    c. What year is it now?   _____

B. *Use the answers from Part A (at the bottom of page 105) to rewrite the sentences. Use* **ago.**

1. Karen washed her car last Saturday. (*Answered as though today is Monday.*)

   Karen washed her car two days ago.

2. Karen learned how to drive in 2005.

   _____

3. Karen visited her high school friends last May.

   _____

4. Karen called her grandparents last Monday.

   _____

5. Karen talked to her parents last Friday.

   _____

6. Karen shared an apartment with friends in 2008.

   _____

7. Karen traveled to Hong Kong last December.

   _____

8. Karen invited some friends for dinner last Wednesday.

   _____

9. Karen worked in Miami in 2009.

   _____

10. Karen started her own business last September.

    _____

EXERCISE 4: Simple Past: Affirmative Statements

Complete the sentences. Use subject pronouns.

1. Pete walks to work every day.

   _____*He walked to work*_____ yesterday too.

2. Lenny, Mike, and Warren play basketball every Saturday.

   _____ last Saturday too.

3. Ellen washes her clothes every Sunday.

_____ last Sunday too.

4. My classmates study every night.

_____ last night too.

5. Robert works in his garden every weekend.

_____ last weekend too.

6. Norman picks up his daughter after school every day.

_____ yesterday too.

7. Anna talks to her son every Friday night.

_____ last Friday night too.

8. Michele and her husband travel to France every summer.

_____ last summer too.

9. The bank closes at 3:00 P.M. every day.

_____ yesterday too.

10. Adam and his sister watch TV every night.

_____ last night too.

EXERCISE 5: Simple Past: Affirmative and Negative Statements

Complete the sentences. Use the correct form of the verbs in parentheses.

1. I _____*watched*_____ TV last night, but I _____*didn't watch*_____ a movie.
      (watch)   (not watch)

2. We _____ our lunch at the hotel yesterday, but we _____
        (enjoy)   (not enjoy)
our dinner.

3. I _____ you on Monday, but I _____ you on Tuesday.
      (email)   (not email)

4. The plane _____ yesterday morning, but it _____ on time.
            (land)   (not land)

5. Monica _____ to call last Saturday, but she _____ to come.
          (promise)   (not promise)

6. We _____ Toronto last year, but we _____ Montreal.
       (visit)   (not visit)

7. Lucy _____ to change her ticket, but she _____ to change
        (try)   (not try)
her husband's ticket.

(continued on next page)

8. We _____ a lot yesterday morning, but we _____ a lot
(walk)   (not walk)

yesterday afternoon.

9. Jerry _____ the meeting yesterday, but he _____ the
(cancel)   (not cancel)

meeting last week.

10. They _____ a car last week, but they _____ a big car.
(rent)   (not rent)

EXERCISE 6: Editing

*Correct the email. There are eight mistakes. The first mistake is already corrected. Find
and correct seven more.*

To: bliu

From: hrseiung

Re: My trip so far

I arrived at the hotel at ten o'clock ~~the~~ last night. I enjoy the flight, but the plane didn't landed on

time. This morning we walked around the town. (We not rent a car because it was very expensive.)

I try to speak Spanish to some of the people in the stores, but they didn't understand me. Ago a few

hours we did visited a very famous park and listen to some great musicians. We're having a really

good time so far.

EXERCISE 7: Personal Writing

Imagine you are a foreigner visiting your city for the first time. Write a postcard about all the interesting places you visited in your city. Use the simple past and at least two time markers.

EXAMPLE: Hi. We arrived in Istanbul two days ago. The weather is beautiful and I'm having a great time. Yesterday Martha and I toured Topkapi Palace and shopped in the Turkish Bazaar. I wanted so many things, but I didn't buy much. Last night we dined at a restaurant on the Bosporus Strait and watched all the boats go by. Istanbul is really a great place to visit!

_____

_____

_____

_____

Simple Past: Affirmative and Negative Statements with Irregular Verbs

EXERCISE 1: Regular and Irregular Verbs

Underline the simple past verb form in each sentence. Write **regular** *if it is regular. Write* **irregular** *if it is irregular. Then write the base form of the verb.*

1. This morning I <u>got</u> up at seven o'clock.   *irregular*   *get*

2. I <u>washed</u> my face and hands.   *regular*   *wash*

3. Then I put on my clothes.   _____   _____

4. I had orange juice and toast for breakfast.   _____   _____

5. After breakfast, I brushed my teeth.   _____   _____

6. I left the house at 7:45.   _____   _____

7. I arrived at school at 8:15.   _____   _____

8. Class began at 8:30.   _____   _____

9. We learned some new grammar rules in class today.   _____   _____

10. Class finished at 11:30.   _____   _____

11. I met some friends for lunch.   _____   _____

12. We ate at a pizza place.   _____   _____

13. After lunch, we went to a swimming pool.   _____   _____

14. We stayed there until five o'clock.   _____   _____

EXERCISE 2: Simple Past of Irregular Verbs: Affirmative Statements

Complete each sentence with the simple past form of the verb.

1. I didn't see Miguel. I _____*saw*_____ Carlos.

2. I didn't get up at 6:00. I _____ up at 7:00.

3. We didn't eat dinner at home. We _____ dinner at a restaurant.

4. She didn't put the bag in the bedroom. She _____ it in the kitchen.

5. Ming didn't go shopping on Saturday. He _____ shopping on Friday.

6. I didn't have eggs for breakfast. I _____ a sandwich.

7. Dr. Wu didn't say that. Dr. Gomez _____ it.

8. Louisa didn't know all the answers. She only _____ three.

9. We didn't meet any people from Mexico, but we _____ people from Peru.

10. Jack didn't come to the party. His wife _____ instead.

11. Adam and Paula didn't sell their TV. They _____ their computer.

12. Mr. Daly didn't teach math. He _____ history.

13. Nick and Jenna didn't leave yesterday. They _____ three days ago.

14. I didn't buy a shirt. I _____ a hat.

15. The movie didn't begin at 8:00. It _____ at 7:45.

EXERCISE 3: Simple Past of Irregular Verbs: Negative Statements

Write true sentences.

1. I / become / an English teacher / last year

   I didn't become an English teacher last year.

2. I / eat / 3 kilos of oranges for breakfast / yesterday morning

_____

3. I / sleep / 21 hours / yesterday

_____

4. I / bring / a horse to English class / two weeks ago

_____

5. I / go / to the moon / last month

_____

6. I / meet / the leader of my country / last night

_____

7. I / find / $10,000 in a brown paper bag / yesterday

_____

(continued on next page)

Simple Past: Affirmative and Negative Statements with Irregular Verbs   **111**

8. I / do / this exercise / two years ago

_____

9. I / swim / 30 kilometers / yesterday

_____

10. I / speak / English perfectly / 10 years ago

_____

EXERCISE 4: Simple Past: Affirmative and Negative Statements

Complete the diary. Use the simple past form of the verbs in parentheses.

I _____had_____ a nice day today. I _____ up until ten
        1. (have)   **2. (not get)**
o'clock, so I _____ dressed quickly and _____ to the
                3. (get)   **4. (go)**
Fine Arts Museum.

    I _____ Cindy and Frank there, and we _____
          5. (meet)   **6. (go)**
into the museum to see a new exhibit. We _____ everything because
                              7. (not see)
we _____ enough time. The exhibit _____ at one o'clock.
      8. (not have)   **9. (close)**
    We _____ at a Chinese restaurant near the museum, and then
          10. (eat)
we _____ a bus to the Downtown Shopping Mall. We
     11. (take)
_____ at the mall for a couple of hours and _____
    12. (stay)   **13. (look)**
around. I _____ a new shirt, but Frank and Cindy
      14. (buy)
_____ anything.
  15. (not buy)
    Cindy and Frank _____ back home with me, and I
                 16. (come)
_____ dinner here. I _____ much in the refrigerator,
  17. (make)   **18. (not have)**
so I _____ to the supermarket to get some things. I
      19. (drive)
_____ Ramón there and _____ him for dinner too.
  20. (see)   **21. (invite)**
    We _____ until late, and after dinner we _____
      22. (not eat)   **23. (watch)**
a DVD. Ramón, Cindy, and Frank _____ until after midnight.
                    24. (not leave)
    It's one o'clock in the morning now, and I'm tired. It's time to go to bed.

Good night!

EXERCISE 5: Editing

Correct the paragraph. There are eight mistakes. The first mistake is already corrected.
Find and correct seven more.

                                    became
Barack Obama ~~become~~ the 44th president of the United States in January 2009. He born in Hawaii in 1961. His father was Kenyan, and his mother was American. They meet at the University of Hawaii and got married, but they didn't stay married for a long time. After his parents divorced, his mother married a man from Indonesia and taked her son to live in Jakarta from the age of six to ten. Then he returned to Hawaii. He spended a lot of time with his grandparents. He graduated from high school in 1979, but he didn't went to college in Hawaii. He leaved Hawaii in 1979 to attend college in California, but he stayed there only two years. Then he go to Columbia University in New York and graduated from there in 1983.

EXERCISE 6: Personal Writing

Write about the life of a family member or friend. Use the simple past.

EXAMPLE: My uncle was a lawyer in Argentina. He left the country for political reasons and came to the United States. In this country, he went back to school and became a librarian. He and my aunt were married for 40 years and had five children. He was very happy with his life. He often said, "I am a lucky man."

_____

_____

_____

_____

UNIT 20 Simple Past: *Yes / No* and *Wh-* Questions

EXERCISE 1: Simple Past: *Yes / No* Questions and Short Answers

Read the information about William Shakespeare. Then read the questions an interviewer asked. Answer the questions. Use short answers.

William Shakespeare, 1564–1616	Place of birth and death: Stratford-upon-Avon, England
Married Anne Hathaway, 1582	Daughter Susanna, born in 1583
Moved to London without family after 1585; worked there as actor and playwright until 1610	Twins Hamnet and Judith, born in 1585
	Wrote over 35 plays and 154 poems

1. Did Shakespeare work in London?   _Yes, he did._

2. Did Shakespeare live in London?   _____

3. Did Shakespeare have any children?   _____

4. Did Shakespeare's family live with him in London?   _____

5. Did Shakespeare write a lot of plays?   _____

6. Did Shakespeare work as an actor?   _____

7. Did Shakespeare's wife have five children?   _____

8. Did Shakespeare die in London?   _____

Look at Sharon's list. Read her conversation with her husband. Write her husband's questions. Then complete each answer. Use the simple past form of the verbs in parentheses.

THINGS TO DO

Get the clothes from the dry cleaners

Buy food for dinner

Meet Glen for lunch

Write a letter to Rena

Go to the bank

Return the book to the library

Look for a birthday present for Jane

Call the doctor

Bake some cookies

Pick the children up at 4:00

SHARON: Steven, you always say I forget to do things. Well, today I remembered to do everything.

STEVEN: Are you sure? Let's see your list. <u>Did you get the clothes from the dry cleaners?</u>
1.

SHARON: Uh-huh. I <u>   put   </u> them in the closet.
2. (put)

STEVEN: _____
3.

SHARON: Yes, I did. I _____ some chicken, some vegetables, and some
4. (get)

apples for dessert.

STEVEN: _____
5.

(continued on next page)

Sharon: Yeah. We _____ at a great Thai restaurant.
6. (eat)

Steven: _____
7.

Sharon: Yes. I _____ it at the post office.
8. (mail)

Steven: _____
9.

Sharon: Yes, I did. I _____ both of the checks.
10. (deposit)

Steven: _____
11.

Sharon: Yes, I did. And I _____ out another book by the same author.
12. (take)

Steven: _____
13.

Sharon: Yeah. I _____ her a sweater.
14. (buy)

Steven: _____
15.

Sharon: Uh-huh. He _____ all the test results are fine.
16. (say)

Steven: _____
17.

Sharon: Of course. And I _____ a few here for you. They're delicious!
18. (have)

Steven: _____
19.

Sharon: Oh no, I _____! What time is it?
20. (forget)

EXERCISE 3: Simple Past: *Wh-* Questions

Match the questions and answers.

__e__ 1. Who wrote *The Merchant of Venice*?

_____ 2. When did the movie *The Merchant of Venice* come out?

_____ 3. Who did you see the movie with?

_____ 4. Why did you want to see the movie?

_____ 5. How long did it take you to read the play?

_____ 6. Who starred in the movie?

_____ 7. Where did you see the movie?

_____ 8. What did you think of the movie?

_____ 9. When did Shakespeare write *The Merchant of Venice*?

a. Al Pacino and Jeremy Irons.

b. My roommate.

c. Hundreds of years ago.

d. At home on a DVD.

e. Shakespeare.

f. In 2005.

g. Because I like the play.

h. It was pretty good.

i. About a month.

Write questions. Use the simple past. Then answer the questions. (If you need help, the answers are at the end of the exercise on page 118, but they are not in order.)

1. Where / Arnold Schwarzenegger / grow up

   Where did Arnold Schwarzenegger grow up?

   In Austria.

2. When / a person / walk on the moon / for the first time

   _____

   _____

3. What / J. K. Rowling / write

   _____

   _____

4. Where / the Olympic Games / start

   _____

   _____

5. Why / many people / go to California / in 1849

   _____

   _____

6. How long / Bill Clinton / live in the White House

   _____

   _____

7. What / Alfred Hitchcock / make

   _____

   _____

8. Why / the Chinese / build the Great Wall

   _____

   _____

(continued on next page)

9. How long / World War II / last in Europe

_____

_____

10. When / Christopher Columbus / sail to / America

_____

_____

About six years.

Eight years.

In 1492.

In 1969.

~~In Austria.~~

In Greece.

Movies.

The *Harry Potter* books.

They wanted to find gold.

They wanted to keep foreigners out of the country.

EXERCISE 5: Questions with *Who* as Subject or Object

Write questions. Use **who** *and the verbs in parentheses.*

1. A: I went to San Francisco during my vacation.

   B: _____ *Who did you go* _____ with?
                       (go)

   A: My friends Adam and Jean.

   B: How did you get there?

   A: By car.

   B: _____ *Who drove* _____?
                   (drive)

   A: We all did.

2. A: Those are beautiful flowers. _____ them to you?
                                                 (give)

   B: My boyfriend.

3. A: I went to a party at my old high school last night.

B: _____ there?
   (see)

A: I saw a few old friends.

4. A: You got a phone call a couple of minutes ago.

B: _____?
   (call)

A: A woman. Her name was Betty Kowalski.

5. A: Did you ever read the book *The Old Man and the Sea*?

B: _____ it?
   (write)

A: Ernest Hemingway.

6. A: Where are the children?

B: At Ryan Santiago's house.

A: _____ them there?
   (take)

B: Ryan's mother.

7. A: My wife sent the money to your office a month ago.

B: _____ it to?
   (send)

A: Nicole Sanda.

8. A: The car is so clean. _____ it?
   (clean)

B: I took it to a car wash.

A: It looks great.

9. A: Did you hear the news? Kay got married.

B: Really? _____?
   (marry)

A: A guy from Oklahoma. I don't know his name.

10. A: My grandparents went to Arizona for two months last winter.

B: _____ with?
   (stay)

A: My cousin, Howard. He has a big house there.

EXERCISE 6: Editing

Correct the conversation. There are six mistakes. The first mistake is already corrected.
Find and correct five more.

                   did you

A: What movie ~~you did~~ see?

B: I went to see *Invictus*.

A: Who did star in it?

B: Matt Damon and Morgan Freeman.

A: Who directed it?

B: Clint Eastwood.

A: What did it be about?

B: It was about Nelson Mandela and his relationship with the coach of the Springboks, the national rugby team of South Africa.

A: When it took place?

B: In the 1990s, after Mandela became president of South Africa.

A: Did you liked the movie?

B: Yes, I did like. My husband liked it too, especially the rugby games.

EXERCISE 7: Personal Writing

You know a friend went to the movies last week. Email your friend about the movie.
Write down questions to ask. Use the simple past.

EXAMPLE: *What movie did you see last week?*
                      Did you like it?

_____

_____

_____

_____

PART VII

VERB REVIEW AND CONTRAST AND EXPANSION

UNIT 21 Simple Past Review

EXERCISE 1: Simple Past: Affirmative and Negative Statements

Complete the sentences. Use the affirmative or negative form of the verbs in parentheses.

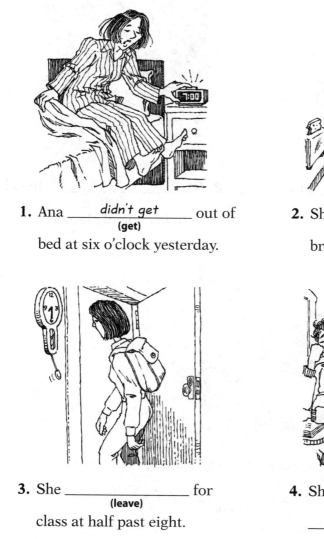

1. Ana ___*didn't get*___ out of
   (get)
   bed at six o'clock yesterday.

2. She _____
   (make)
   breakfast.

3. She _____ for
   (leave)
   class at half past eight.

4. She and her classmates

   _____ all tired.
   (be)

(continued on next page)

5. She _____ lunch
  (have)
alone.

6. In the afternoon, she

_____ golf.
  (play)

7. She _____ some
  (buy)
dog food.

8. She _____ dinner
  (eat)
with her friend Marcia.

9. After dinner, she and her dog

Rocky _____ TV.
  (watch)

EXERCISE 2: Simple Past: *Yes / No* Questions and Short Answers

Answer the questions. Use short answers.

1. Did you use this book last year? _No, I didn't._

2. Were your parents born in New York? _____

3. Did you buy anything yesterday? _____

4. Was your father a good student? _____

5. Was it cold yesterday? _____

6. Did you take a shower yesterday? _____

7. Were you born in a hospital? _____

8. Did your parents get married five years ago? _____

9. Did you and a friend go to the movies last night? _____

10. Was the last grammar exercise easy? _____

11. Did your English teacher give you a test last week? _____

12. Were you absent from your last English class? _____

EXERCISE 3: Past of *Be*: *Yes / No* Questions and Answers

Write questions and answers. Use the simple past of **be.**

1. **A:** _Was George Washington a soldier?_ (George Washington / a soldier)

   B: _Yes, he was a soldier and president._ (yes / he / a soldier and president)

2. **A:** _____ (you / good at history in school)

   B: _____ (yes / it / my favorite subject)

3. **A:** _____ (your history books / interesting)

   B: _____ (they / OK)

4. **A:** _____ (you / a talkative child)

   B: _____ (no / I / very quiet)

5. **A:** _____ (your parents / born in the United States)

   B: _____ (no / they / born in Colombia)

(continued on next page)

6. **A:** _____ (your mother / born in 1942)

   B: _____ (yes / she / born in May 1942)

7. **A:** _____ (Michael Jordan / a great baseball player)

   B: _____ (no / he / a great basketball player)

8. **A:** _____ (the movie about Ray Charles / good)

   B: _____ (yes / the actor / outstanding)

EXERCISE 4: Simple Past: *Wh-* Questions

Complete the conversations. Circle the correct questions and write them on the lines.

1. **A:** I was absent yesterday.

   B: *What was wrong?* _____

      a. Who was absent?   **(b.)** What was wrong?

   A: I was ill.

2. **A:** We had dinner at the new Mexican restaurant.

   B: _____

      a. How was the food?   **b.** Did you like the food?

   A: Yes. It was very good.

3. **A:** You forgot Cathy's birthday.

   B: _____

      a. When was it?   **b.** Where was she?

   A: Last Thursday.

4. **A:** I went to bed at eight o'clock last night.

   B: _____

      a. What did you do?   **b.** Why were you so tired?

   A: I don't know. I didn't feel very well.

5. A: You missed a great party.

B: _____

    a. Who was there?   **b.** How was the party?

A: People from our class and their friends.

6. A: I found your keys.

B: _____

    a. Where did you find them?   **b.** Why were they there?

A: Under the desk.

7. A: I got everything right on the test.

B: _____

    a. Really? Where were the answers to the first and third questions?

    b. Really? What were the answers to the first and third questions?

A: The answer to the first was C, and D was the answer to the third.

8. A: We were on vacation for two weeks.

B: _____

    a. Where did you go?   **b.** How was it?

A: It was great.

9. A: We had a great time in Hong Kong.

B: _____

    a. Who were you with?   **b.** When did you go there?

A: We were there about two years ago.

10. A: I went to a great movie with Andrea last night.

B: _____

    a. Why didn't you call me and see if I wanted to go?

    b. Why did you go with Andrea and not me?

A: I did, but you weren't home.

EXERCISE 5: Simple Past: *Wh-* Questions

Complete the questions. Use **was**, **were**, *or* **did**. *Then match the questions and answers.*

   e   1. Where ___*did*___ you go on vacation?

_____ 2. When _____ the flight from New York?

_____ 3. What _____ you see?

_____ 4. How _____ the weather?

_____ 5. Where _____ you stay?

_____ 6. How _____ you travel around Turkey?

_____ 7. Who _____ with you?

_____ 8. When _____ your vacation?

_____ 9. How _____ the restaurants?

_____ 10. Why _____ you go there?

_____ 11. Who _____ you meet?

_____ 12. What _____ your favorite place?

a. My friend Ginny.

b. It was fine, but it rained a few times.

c. By plane and bus.

d. Istanbul.

e. Turkey.

f. I always wanted to go to Turkey.

g. At different hotels.

h. On May 10th.

i. Many interesting things.

j. Some people in the hotels.

k. Great—Turkish food is delicious.

l. In May.

EXERCISE 6: Past of *Be*: *Wh-* Questions

Complete the conversations. Write correct questions.

1. **A:** Did you pay a lot of money for those sunglasses?

   B: No, they were on sale.

   A: When _*were they on sale*_____?

   B: Last week.

2. **A:** I tried to call you last night.

   B: I wasn't home.

   A: Where _____?

   B: At a friend's apartment.

3. **A:** Did you have your history test yesterday?

   B: No, we had it today.

   A: How _____?

   B: It was OK, but I didn't know the answers to two of the questions.

4. A: Did the kids go swimming?

   B: No, they were afraid.

   A: Why _____?

   B: The water was deep.

5. A: Did you go to the basketball game?

   B: Yeah, it was a great game.

   A: What _____?

   B: I don't remember the score, but our team won.

6. A: Those are beautiful shoes. Where did you get them?

   B: At a store on Washington Street.

   A: What _____?

   B: I think the name of the store was Dalton's. Or was it Dillon's?

7. A: Did your dog have her puppies yet?

   B: She sure did—six of them.

   A: When _____?

   B: They were born a few days ago.

8. A: What's new?

   B: The police were here.

   A: Why _____?

   B: Someone called them, but I don't know why.

9. A: You were brave to go there alone.

   B: I wasn't alone.

   A: Who _____?

   B: My brother and sister.

10. A: Did you ever read this book?

   B: Yes, it was about Eleanor Roosevelt.

   A: Who _____?

   B: She was the wife of President Franklin Roosevelt.

EXERCISE 7: Editing

Correct the conversation. There are nine mistakes. The first mistake is already corrected. Find and correct eight more.

               did

A: Where you grow up?

B: In Montreal. I am born in Morocco, but I not live there for a long time, only two years.

A: Did you liked life in Montreal?

B: I loved it. It was home. But it not be easy for my parents. They always missed life in Morocco, especially the weather.

A: Why were you move to New York?

B: I went to college here and then I get a job, so I didn't went back to Canada.

A: Where are your parents now?

B: My father died before five years, and my mother is back in Morocco with her sisters.

EXERCISE 8: Personal Writing

Write a biography of a grandparent or great grandparent or another relative who is no longer alive. Use the simple past.

EXAMPLE: My great grandmother was born in Philadelphia, Pennsylvania, in 1919. She married in 1940 and had three children. She was always a very independent woman. After my great grandfather died in 1952, she took over his business and ran it very successfully. Late in life, she took up painting. She was a talented artist, and she sold a number of her paintings. She also loved poetry and loved to recite poems. She really was an amazing woman.

_____

_____

_____

_____

_____

UNIT 22 Gerunds and Infinitives

EXERCISE 1: Verbs

Match the sentences with the speakers.

_h_ **1.** I keep telling Ms. Fox that she needs rest.

_____ **2.** I enjoy fixing things.

_____ **3.** I can't stand cleaning all the time!

_____ **4.** All of you need to study more.

_____ **5.** We're very competitive; we intend to win.

_____ **6.** Do you want to order something to drink?

_____ **7.** I hope to speak English perfectly one day.

_____ **8.** I avoid playing the piano late at night.

_____ **9.** I prefer working in the movies to working in television.

a. a language student

b. an athlete

c. a waiter

d. an actor

e. a musician

f. a maid

g. a mechanic

h. a doctor

i. a teacher

EXERCISE 2: Infinitives and Gerunds

*Make sentences with **love**, **enjoy**, and **hate**. Use an infinitive or gerund.*

☺ = **love**	☺ = **enjoy**	☹ = **hate**

1. Tom— ☺ —meet new people   *Tom enjoys meeting new people.*

2. Terry— ☹ —travel   _____

3. Marsha— ☺ —take photographs   _____

4. Elena— ☺ —write poems   _____

5. Steve— ☺ —be on an airplane   _____

6. Dana— ☺ —speak other languages   _____

7. Rena— ☹ —work in an office   _____

8. Leo— ☺ —learn new things   _____

EXERCISE 3: Verbs Plus Infinitives and Gerunds

Complete the sentences. Write the correct form of the verbs from the box.

be	do	move	relax	swim
~~buy~~	help	receive	study	talk

1. **A:** Why are you going to the store?

   B: I want _____to buy_____ some fruit.

2. **A:** Why do you go to the swimming pool on Sunday mornings?

   B: I prefer _____ on Sundays. It's quiet then.

3. **A:** Why are you angry with your roommate?

   B: She never wants _____ with the housework.

4. **A:** Why are you closing the door?

   B: I need _____ to you in private.

5. **A:** Why are Gina and Louis looking for an apartment?

   B: They want _____.

6. **A:** Why are they going to the airport so late?

   B: They do not need _____ at the airport until the evening.

7. **A:** Why do you write so many letters?

   B: Because we like _____ them.

8. **A:** Why do you go to the library after class every day?

   B: I prefer _____ my homework there.

9. **A:** Why do you and your wife always stay home on Sundays?

   B: We like _____ one day a week.

10. **A:** Why are you putting your books away?

    B: Because I finished _____ for the test.

EXERCISE 4: Editing

Correct the conversation. There are six mistakes. The first mistake is already corrected.
Find and correct five more.

                                       going

A: Are you thinking about ~~go~~ to graduate school?

B: Yes, I want be a software developer, so I need to get a master's degree.

A: Where do you plan working?

B: I don't know. I'm getting tired of live here, so I'm thinking about moving to Chicago.

A: Why Chicago?

B: I was born there, and I always enjoy to visit the city. What about you? What are

    your plans?

A: Oh, I don't know. I avoid to think about the future.

EXERCISE 5: Personal Writing

Write about yourself as a language learner. Use gerunds and infinitives. Talk about
these things, or your own ideas:

- Your likes and dislikes about learning English
- Your learning strategies
- Your hopes and/or plans

EXAMPLE: *I really want to speak English well, so every day I try to learn five new words. I*
write them down on flashcards and look at them at different times of the day. In
class, I avoid speaking to people from my country. I speak more English that way.
I really enjoy being in a class with people from different countries, and I hope to
take another English class.

_____

_____

_____

_____

EXERCISE 1: Simple Present, Present Progressive, Simple Past: Time Expressions

Complete the sentences with the correct tense of the verbs in parentheses.

1. These days I _____*'m living*_____ (live) with a roommate. We

   usually _____ (have) meals together. Last night we

   _____ (eat) at a very nice restaurant.

2. I _____ (have) a great time at the beach two days ago. I

   _____ (not go) to the beach very often. I don't think anyone is

   at the beach right now. It _____ (be) raining.

3. Why _____ (you / do) that now? Yesterday morning

   I _____ (tell) you not to do that again. You never

   _____ (listen) to me!

4. I _____ (move) here a few years ago, but I

   _____ (not live) here all the time. I spend every summer with

   my family in Haiti. I _____ (write) to you from there right now.

5. My parents _____ (give) me a smart phone for my

   birthday last year. At first, I used it only for phone calls, but these days I

   _____ (use) it for all kinds of things. It's strange, but I hardly

   ever _____ (make) phone calls with it now.

EXERCISE 2: Simple Present, Present Progressive, Simple Past: Affirmative

Change the negative statements to positive statements.

1. He doesn't have many new ideas.

   *He has many new ideas.*_____.

2. Scientists aren't coming up with new ways to use these medicines.

   _____.

3. I didn't sleep well last night.

   _____.

4. She didn't reject all of our ideas.

   _____.

5. They're not inventing new uses for the phone.

   _____.

EXERCISE 3: Simple Present, Present Progressive, Simple Past: Negative

Change the positive statements to negative statements.

1. He enjoys doing research.

   *He doesn't enjoy doing research.*_____.

2. I'm thinking about their plans for the future.

   _____.

3. The teacher gives homework every day.

   _____.

4. We accepted all of their suggestions.

   _____.

5. They discovered a cure for that disease.

   _____.

Complete the sentences with the correct form of the verbs in parentheses.

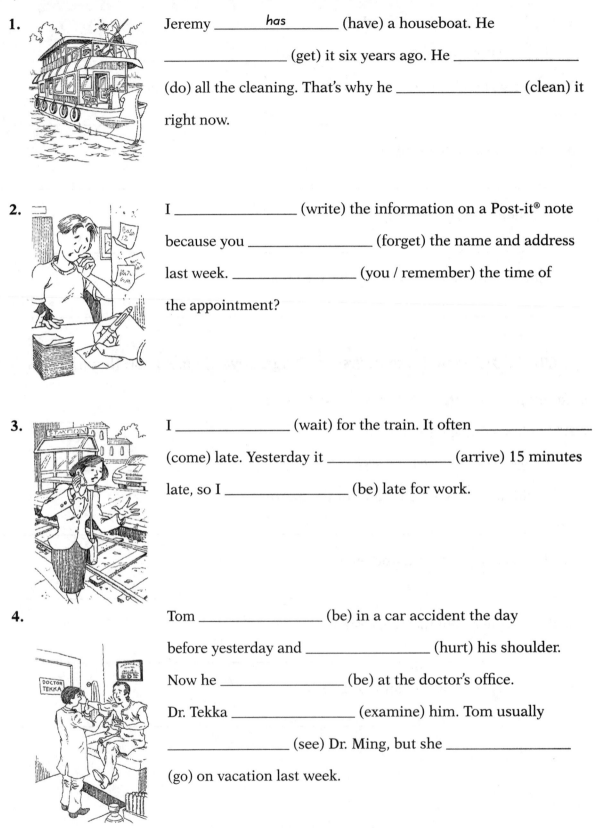

1. Jeremy _____ *has* _____ (have) a houseboat. He

   _____ (get) it six years ago. He _____

   (do) all the cleaning. That's why he _____ (clean) it

   right now.

2. I _____ (write) the information on a Post-it® note

   because you _____ (forget) the name and address

   last week. _____ (you / remember) the time of

   the appointment?

3. I _____ (wait) for the train. It often _____

   (come) late. Yesterday it _____ (arrive) 15 minutes

   late, so I _____ (be) late for work.

4. Tom _____ (be) in a car accident the day

   before yesterday and _____ (hurt) his shoulder.

   Now he _____ (be) at the doctor's office.

   Dr. Tekka _____ (examine) him. Tom usually

   _____ (see) Dr. Ming, but she _____

   (go) on vacation last week.

5.

Tonya and Roy _____ (have) dinner late tonight.

They usually _____ (eat) at around six o'clock, but

the children _____ (be) at a birthday party and

_____ (not come) home until 6:30.

6.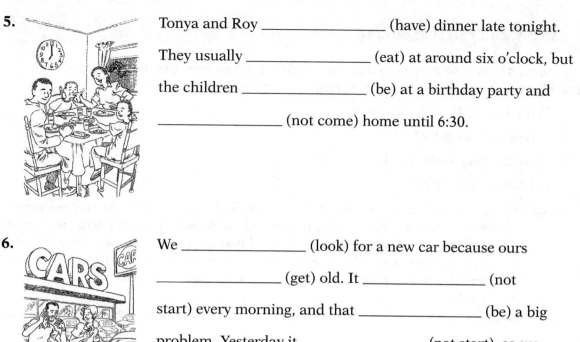

We _____ (look) for a new car because ours

_____ (get) old. It _____ (not

start) every morning, and that _____ (be) a big

problem. Yesterday it _____ (not start), so we

_____ (take) the subway to work.

EXERCISE 5: Editing

Correct the conversation. There are six mistakes. The first mistake is already corrected.
Find and correct five more.

         want
A: I ~~am wanting~~ to pay for these things.

B: Do you pay with cash or a credit card?

A: Credit. Here's my card.

B: You forget to sign the back of it.

A: Really? I didn't know that. I am using it just a few minutes ago and the cashier

    doesn't say anything.

B: Oh, people are doing it all the time.

EXERCISE 6: Personal Writing

Write about a device, such as a smart phone or a GPS, that you own. Use the simple present, present progressive, and simple past. Answer these questions:

- Who invented it? (if you know)
- When did you get it?
- How do you usually use it?
- Are you using it now?

EXAMPLE: *Last year I got a new smart phone. I made phone calls and sent text messages with my old cell phone. I use my smart phone to make calls and send messages too, but I also use it for many other things. I take photos and go online with it. I also check my email and listen to music on it. Sometimes I find directions with it. I'm not using it now. I'm doing this exercise with a pen in my workbook.*

_____

_____

_____

_____

_____

UNIT 24 *Be going to* for the Future

EXERCISE 1: Future Time Markers

*Rewrite the sentences. Replace the underlined words with another future time expression. Use **tonight** or combine the correct words from each column.*

next	week
this	month
tomorrow	morning
	afternoon
	night
	evening

(It's eight o'clock in the morning on Saturday, April 7th.)

1. The president of our college is going to speak about the plans <u>in one hour</u>.

   The president of our college is going to speak about the plans this morning.

2. The professors are going to give their opinion about the plans <u>in 10 hours</u>.

   _____

3. The students are probably going to protest the plans <u>in 36 hours</u>.

   _____

4. The architects are going to present new plans for the campus <u>in one week</u>.

   _____

5. The workers are going to start work on the new building <u>in one month</u>.

   _____

6. A story about new buildings on campus is going to be on TV <u>in 14 hours</u>.

   _____

7. We are going to take a tour of the new arts center <u>in seven hours</u>.

   _____

EXERCISE 2: Future Time Markers

*Rewrite the sentences. Replace the underlined words with another future time expression. Use **in**.*

(It is two o'clock in the afternoon on Monday, October 13th.)

1. Max is going to attend a meeting <u>at four o'clock this afternoon</u>.

   Max is going to attend a meeting in two hours.

2. Max is going to leave the office <u>at 2:15 this afternoon</u>.

   _____

3. Max and Debbie are going to get married <u>on April 13th</u>.

   _____

4. Debbie is going to start a new job <u>on October 27th</u>.

   _____

5. Debbie is going to take Max to her parents' home <u>on Friday, October 17th</u>.

   _____

EXERCISE 3: Future Plans

*What are your plans for tomorrow? Put a check (✓) next to the things you are probably going to do. Put an **X** next to the things you are definitely not going to do.*

_____ **1.** study

_____ **2.** go shopping

_____ **3.** take pictures

_____ **4.** watch TV

_____ **5.** go out with friends

_____ **6.** listen to music

_____ **7.** visit relatives

_____ **8.** talk on the telephone

_____ **9.** take a shower

_____ **10.** check my email

_____ **11.** go skiing

_____ **12.** stay home

EXERCISE 4: *Be going to*: Affirmative and Negative Statements

Write six true sentences about your plans for tomorrow. Use the information from Exercise 3.

EXAMPLE:

__✓__ study   __X__ visit relatives

I am going to study tomorrow.

I am not going to visit relatives tomorrow.

1. _____

2. _____

3. _____

4. _____

5. _____

6. _____

EXERCISE 5: *Be going to*: Affirmative Statements

*Some people are going out. What are they going to do? Make guesses and write sentences with **be going to**.*

Nora is taking a cell phone and car keys.

1. She's going to talk on the phone. _____

2. _____

Jessica and Peter Greblo are taking a suitcase and a camera.

3. _____

4. _____

David is taking a DVD and a textbook.

5. _____

6. _____

EXERCISE 6: *Be going to*: Negative Statements

Write sentences about the future. Use **not** *and* **be going to.**

1. It's Wednesday morning. Reggie usually plays tennis on Wednesday afternoon, but he has a bad cold.

   _____*He isn't* (OR *He's not*) *going to play*_____ tennis this afternoon.

2. It's July. Joan usually takes a vacation in August, but she has money problems this year.

   _____ a vacation this August.

3. Mary always takes a shower in the morning, but there's no hot water today.

   _____ a shower this morning.

4. It's eleven o'clock in the morning. The children usually play outside after lunch, but the weather is terrible today.

   _____ outside this afternoon.

5. It's six o'clock. Carl and his wife usually watch television after dinner, but there's nothing good on television.

   _____ television tonight.

6. It's eleven o'clock. I usually eat lunch around noon, but I finished a big breakfast at 10:30.

   _____ lunch at noon today.

7. It's 12 noon. My friend and I like to swim on Saturday afternoons, but my friend went away for the weekend and I'm tired.

   _____ this afternoon.

8. It's nine o'clock in the morning. Dr. Morita usually sees patients at his office every morning, but there's an emergency at the hospital. He can't leave until noon.

   _____ patients at his office this morning.

9. I usually wake up at six o'clock in the morning, but tomorrow is a holiday.

   _____ at six o'clock tomorrow morning.

10. It's ten o'clock in the morning. The letter carrier usually delivers all the mail by one o'clock, but he started late this morning.

    _____ all the mail by one o'clock today.

Write questions. Use **be going to.**

1. What / he / make

   What is he going to make? _____

2. Who / cook / tonight

   _____

3. When / dinner / be / ready

   _____

4. Why / he / cook / so much food

   _____

5. How long / he / need / to cook the dinner

   _____

6. Who / come

   _____

7. How / he / cook / the lamb

   _____

8. Where / all of your guests / sit

   _____

9. What / you / do

   _____

10. How long / your guests / stay

    _____

EXERCISE 8: *Be going to*: *Wh-* Questions

Write the correct questions from Exercise 7.

1. **A:** Who is going to cook tonight?

   B: My husband.

2. **A:** _____

   B: Soup, salad, lamb, potatoes, some vegetables, and dessert.

3. **A:** _____

   B: We're going to have a dinner party.

4. **A:** _____

   B: He's going to roast it in the oven.

5. **A:** _____

   B: About 15 of our relatives.

6. **A:** _____

   B: My husband's fast. Probably two or three hours.

7. **A:** _____

   B: I'm going to wash the dishes.

8. **A:** _____

   B: At around seven o'clock.

9. **A:** _____

   B: They're going to come at 6:00 and probably stay until about 11:00.

10. **A:** _____

    B: My sister's going to bring extra chairs.

EXERCISE 9: Present Progressive for Now and for Future

Underline the verb in each sentence. Write **now** *if the speaker is talking about now.*
Write **future** *if the speaker is talking about the future.*

1. Where <u>is</u> he <u>going</u> next week?   _____future_____

2. Where <u>is</u> he <u>going</u>?   _____now_____

3. I'm doing my homework.   _____

4. We're not having a meeting on Monday. _____

5. They're moving in three weeks. _____

6. Are you having dinner? _____

7. Are you leaving soon? _____

8. The children are not sleeping. _____

9. Where are you going on the weekend? _____

10. Why is he coming? _____

EXERCISE 10: Present Progressive for Future

Roger and Helen are taking a trip to Great Britain. Here is their schedule. Write sentences about their future activities. Use the present progressive.

May 8	6:00 P.M.	Meet your group at the airport
	7:30	Fly to London
May 9	6:45 A.M.	Arrive in London
May 9 and 10		Stay at the London Regency Hotel
May 9	2:00 P.M.	Visit Buckingham Palace
	4:30	Have tea at the Ritz Hotel
	7:30	Go to the theater
May 10	9:00 A.M.	Go on a tour of central London
	12:00 P.M.	Eat lunch at a typical English pub
May 11	8:00 A.M.	Leave for Scotland

1. *They are meeting their group at the airport at 6:00 P.M. on May 8.* _____

2. _____

3. _____

4. _____

5. _____

6. _____

7. _____

8. _____

9. _____

10. _____

Write questions. Use the present progressive. Then write short answers.

1. you / meet / friends / tomorrow

   Are you meeting friends tomorrow?   Yes, I am. OR No, I'm not.

2. you / go / shopping / this weekend

   _____   _____

3. you / work / next week

   _____   _____

4. your friend / have / a party / next Saturday

   _____   _____

5. your classmates / study / with you / tonight

   _____   _____

6. your neighbor / come / to your place / tomorrow

   _____   _____

7. your parents / move / next year

   _____   _____

8. your classmates / have / dinner together / tomorrow

   _____   _____

9. you and your friends / go to the movies / on the weekend

   _____   _____

10. your teacher / make / lunch for you / tomorrow

   _____   _____

Ask Stephanie about her vacation plans. Write questions. Use a word from each column and the present progressive.

Why		stay
When		take
Where		go
Who	you	go with
How long		leave
What		drive
How		get there

1. *Where are you going?*

   To Colorado.

2. _____

   On September 16th.

3. _____

   By car.

4. _____

   Airplane tickets are too expensive.

5. _____

   Two weeks.

6. _____

   Some friends from college.

7. _____

   A tent, sleeping bags, and bikes.

EXERCISE 13: Editing

Correct the conversation. There are seven mistakes. The first mistake is already corrected. Find and correct six more.

        Is the

A: ~~The~~ mayor going to meet with the police chief this morning?

B: No, he isn't going. He goes to meet with the Parents' and Teachers' Association.

They're going to talk about conditions in the schools. Then he's going to having lunch

with a group of community leaders.

A: What they are going to discuss?

B: I don't know. But they aren't being happy with the budget for next year. There's going

be less money for all the neighborhood centers!

EXERCISE 14: Personal Writing

*Write about changes in your life in the near future. Use **be going to** for the future.*

EXAMPLE: *I'm going to graduate from college next May, and I'm probably going to move to Los Angeles. I have some relatives there, so in the beginning, I'm going to stay with them. I hope to find a good job because I don't want to live with my family for a long time. I'm going to look for a job in city planning. I studied architecture in school, and that's my dream.*

_____

_____

_____

_____

_____

EXERCISE 1: *Will*: Affirmative Statements

*Complete the conversations. Use **I'll** and the words from the box.*

close the window	get you some aspirin	help you	turn on the air conditioner
drive you	get you some water	make you a sandwich	wash them

1. **A** I'm cold.

    B: _I'll close the window._

2. **A:** I'm thirsty.

    B: _____

3. **A:** I can't lift this box.

    B: _____

4. **A:** I'm hot.

    B: _____

5. **A:** I'm hungry.

    B: _____

6. **A:** I have a headache.

    B: _____

7. **A:** I'm late for class.

    B: _____

8. **A:** There are dirty dishes in the sink.

    B: _____

EXERCISE 2: *Will*: Contractions

By the year 2050, many things in our lives will change. Rewrite the sentences. Replace the bold words with contractions.

1. On average, people will be taller than they are today. **They will** also weigh more.

   On average, people will be taller than they are today. They'll also weigh more.

2. Scientists will find cures for many diseases. **We will not** get sick as often.

   _____

3. Many more people will live to be 100 years old. **They will** also be healthier.

   _____

4. **We will not** use paper money and coins for our purchases. **We will** use credit cards.

   _____

5. Robots will cook our meals and clean our homes. **We will** have a lot more leisure time.

   _____

6. Cars will run on solar energy. **They will not** use gasoline.

   _____

7. Travel to the moon will be common. **We will** go to the moon on vacation!

   _____

EXERCISE 3: *Will*: Contractions

Here are some affirmative sentences about future events. Write them with contractions. Then make them negative.

1. We will see you tomorrow. *We'll see you tomorrow. / We won't see you tomorrow.*

2. You will be very happy there. _____

3. I will be there early. _____

4. She will do it. _____

5. It will be hot tomorrow. _____

6. They will come to the meeting. _____

7. He will get the job. _____

Complete the sentences. Circle the correct answers and write them on the lines.

1. **A:** What's the weather forecast for tomorrow?

   B: The newspaper says it _____ will snow _____.

   a. is snowing   (**b.**) will snow

2. **A:** Where are you going with the soap and water?

   B: I _____ wash the car.

   a. am going to   **b.** will

3. **A:** Do you see my umbrella?

   B: Yes, it's over there. I _____ get it for you.

   a. am going to   **b.** will

4. **A:** Why is Myra so happy these days?

   B: She _____ get married.

   a. is going to   **b.** will

5. **A:** Why _____ see that film?

   a. are you going to   **b.** will you

   B: I heard it was good.

6. **A:** The dishwasher isn't working. I'm going to call the repairman.

   B: No, don't. I _____ it.

   a. am fixing   **b.** will fix

7. **A:** I think men _____ dresses in the future.

   a. are wearing   **b.** will wear

   B: You're crazy!

8. **A:** _____ anything this weekend?

   a. Are you doing   **b.** Will you do

   B: I'm not sure yet. Why?

9. **A:** _____ everything by computer in 50 years?

   a. Are people buying   **b.** Will people buy

   B: Maybe.

EXERCISE 5: *Will*: Negative Statements

Write negative sentences with the same meaning.

1. Cars will be small.

   Cars won't be big.

2. I'll leave early.

   _____

3. It'll be cold.

   _____

4. Coffee will cost less.

   _____

5. People will spend more time with their families.

   _____

6. We will come after seven o'clock.

   _____

7. Mr. and Mrs. McNamara will buy an old car.

   _____

8. Valerie will win the game.

   _____

9. The parking lot will be empty.

   _____

EXERCISE 6: *Will*: Affirmative and Negative Statements and *Yes / No* and *Wh-* Questions

*A fortune teller is telling Mark about his future. Complete the conversation. Use **will** or **won't** and the words in parentheses.*

FORTUNE TELLER: Your future _____*will be*_____ a happy one.
                                  1. (be)

MARK: _____ rich?
         2. (I / be)

FORTUNE TELLER: Yes. You _____ a very rich woman.
                            3. (marry)

MARK: Where _____ her?
4. (I / meet)

FORTUNE TELLER: That I can't tell you, but it _____ love at first sight.
5. (be)

MARK: _____ me forever?
6. (she / love)

FORTUNE TELLER: Forever.

MARK: When _____?
7. (we / meet)

FORTUNE TELLER: Soon.

MARK: What about children?

FORTUNE TELLER: You _____ many children—just two, a boy and
8. (not have)

a girl.

MARK: That's a good number. What else?

FORTUNE TELLER: You _____ famous.
9. (be)

MARK: Really? Why _____ famous?
10. (I / be)

FORTUNE TELLER: I'm not sure, but it _____ fun for you. People
11. (not be)

_____ you all the time.
12. (bother)

MARK: Oh! I _____ that. _____
13. (not like)   14. (our home / have)

everything?

FORTUNE TELLER: Yes, everything.

MARK: Good. Then we _____ it, and people
15. (not leave)

_____ us.
16. (not bother)

FORTUNE TELLER: But then you _____ a prisoner in your own home.
17. (become)

_____ you happy?
18. (that / make)

MARK: Oh, why isn't life perfect?

FORTUNE TELLER: That I cannot tell you.

Complete the sentences. Choose the present, the past, or the future with **will**. Use the verbs in parentheses.

Well, here I am on the moon. We _____ *arrived* _____ a few hours ago. First, I
1. (arrive)

_____ a walk on the moon. It _____ so strange. Then
2. (take)   3. (be)

we _____ something, but it _____ normal food. Right
4. (eat)   5. (be not)

now we _____. Of course, we _____ and we
6. (rest)   7. (not sit)

_____ down. This is outer space and people _____
8. (not lie)   9. (not sit)

here. And they _____ down here either. We _____ here
10. (not lie)   11. (be)

for three more days. Then we _____ to Earth. It _____
12. (return)   13. (not be)

a long trip, but I'm sure it _____ fun.
14. (be)

EXERCISE 8: Editing

Correct the conversation. There are six mistakes. The first mistake is already corrected.
Find and correct five more.

  A: Things will ~~are~~ *be* different next year.

  B: How will be they different?

  A: Well, for one thing, I won't to be in school any more. I won't takes any more exams,

   and I'll have lots of free time.

  B: Will you have a job?

  A: Yes, I'll. I hope to have a very good job.

  B: Then how will you lots of free time?

  A: It'll be a different kind of free time.

EXERCISE 9: Personal Writing

Write about how your life will be better in 25 years' time and / or how it will be worse.
Use **will** *for the future.*

  EXAMPLE: Twenty-five years from now I will be forty-eight years old. I'll probably be married
   and have a couple of children. My life will be better because I will have a job and
   I'll have more money. Of course, it will be nice to have a family too. But I'll have to
   work all the time in order to support my family, and my children probably won't
   listen to me all the time. In that way, my life will be worse.

  _____

  _____

  _____

  _____

UNIT 26 *May* or *Might* for Possibility

May or *Might* for Possibility

EXERCISE 1: *May* and *Might* for Possibility

*Put a check (✓) next to the sentences that are possible where you live. Put an **X** next to the sentences that are not possible.*

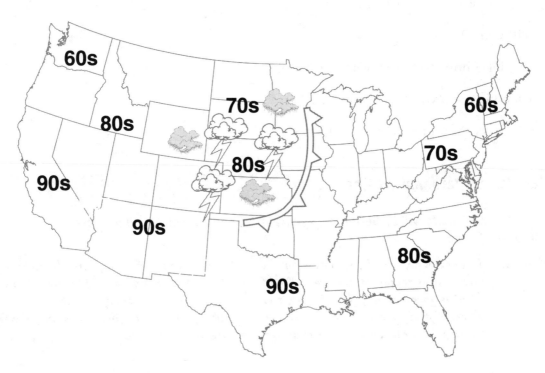

_____ **1.** It might rain tomorrow.

_____ **2.** It may snow next month.

_____ **3.** It may not be sunny tomorrow.

_____ **4.** It might be windy next week.

_____ **5.** It might be very cold on the weekend.

_____ **6.** It may be 37° Celsius (98.6° F) next month.

_____ **7.** It may be very hot tomorrow.

_____ **8.** It might be windy next week.

_____ **9.** It might not be mild tomorrow morning.

_____ **10.** It might be −5° Celsius (23° F) tonight.

Rewrite the sentences. Use **may** *or* **might**.

1. Maybe there will be a storm.

   There may be a storm. OR *There might be a storm.*

2. Perhaps they won't listen to the weather report.

   _____

3. Perhaps he won't drive in the snow.

   _____

4. Maybe they will stay home.

   _____

5. Perhaps she will go to the beach.

   _____

6. Maybe we won't ride our bikes in the hot weather.

   _____

7. Maybe you will need a hat.

   _____

8. Perhaps there will be flooding on the highway.

   _____

9. Maybe the weather report will be wrong.

   _____

10. Perhaps the weather will improve.

    _____

EXERCISE 3: *Will* for Definite Future and *May* for Possibility

Complete the sentences. Use **may** *or* **will**.

1. Tomorrow is my birthday. I _____*will*_____ be twenty-five.

2. I'm tall. My children _____*may*_____ be tall too.

3. I don't know anything about that movie. It _____ not be good.

(continued on next page)

4. Are you taking a trip to the United States? You _____ need a passport. Everybody from Brazil needs one.

5. Don't worry. I _____ do it. I promise.

6. Ask about the price. It _____ be expensive.

7. The commute _____ be bad, but I'm not sure.

8. There's someone at the door. I _____ open it.

9. The sun _____ rise tomorrow.

10. The food _____ be ready. I'm going to look.

EXERCISE 4: *May* and *Might*: Affirmative and Negative Statements

Complete the sentences. Use **may (not)** *or* **might (not)** *and the words from the box.*

bite	close	get lost	have an accident	~~pass~~
break	~~fall~~	get sick	live	win

1. Janet is worried about her little boy. He's climbing a tree.

He *may fall. (OR might fall.)* _____

2. Jimmy has a test today, and he didn't study.

He *may not pass. (OR might not pass.)* _____

3. Lynn is driving fast.

She _____

4. Wrap those glasses carefully.

They _____

5. Mark Muller is one of the top tennis players in the world, but he isn't playing well today.

He _____

6. Don't lose these directions. It's difficult to find my house.

You _____

7. The woman's injuries are very bad.

She _____

8. Don't go near that animal.

It _____

9. Don't go outside with wet hair. It's cold.

You _____

10. That store never has many customers.

It _____

EXERCISE 5: Editing

Correct the conversation. There are six mistakes. The first mistake is already corrected.
Find and correct five more.

     I may go

A: ~~Maybe I go~~ to the movies tonight.

B: Take your umbrella. It may rains. What are you going to see?

A: I don't know. I'll see the new Sam Fong movie. I heard good things about it. Do you

want to come?

B: I can't. I'm waiting for a call from Dana. We might to study together tonight.

A: On a Saturday night?

B: It's the only free time I have. I mightn't be around next week.

A: Why? Where may you be?

B: Working in my father's store. He might have to go in the hospital for a few days, but

we're not sure yet.

EXERCISE 6: Personal Writing

Write about your plans for next weekend. Will it rain? Will it be sunny? Talk about what is definite and what is possible. Use **may** *and* **might** *where possible.*

EXAMPLE: It might rain on Saturday, so I won't go to the beach. I'll go shopping downtown in the morning. In the afternoon, I'll help my father clean the garage. On Saturday evening, I'll get together with my friends. First, we'll go out to eat. Then we'll go to the movies or we may just hang out. On Sunday, I'll visit my grandparents. It will be sunny, so we may go to the park. In the evening after dinner, I'll do my homework for class the next day.

_____

_____

_____

_____

_____

UNIT 27 Count and Non-Count Nouns, Quantifiers, Articles

EXERCISE 1: Count Nouns and Non-Count Nouns

Look at the store signs. Write the correct aisle number.

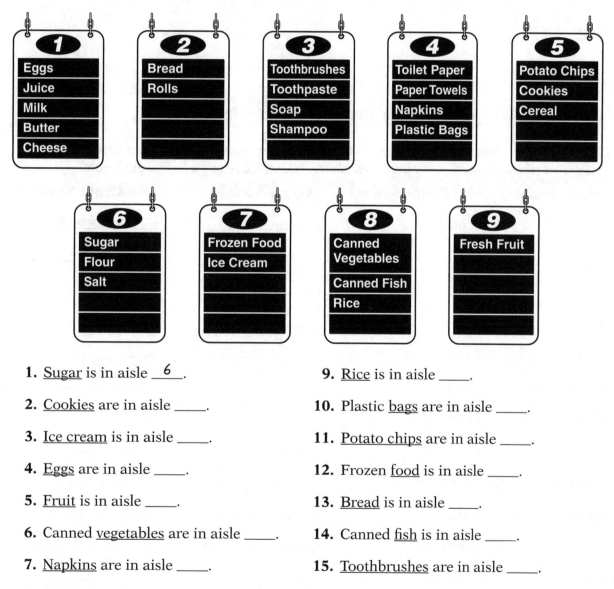

1 Eggs / Juice / Milk / Butter / Cheese

2 Bread / Rolls

3 Toothbrushes / Toothpaste / Soap / Shampoo

4 Toilet Paper / Paper Towels / Napkins / Plastic Bags

5 Potato Chips / Cookies / Cereal

6 Sugar / Flour / Salt

7 Frozen Food / Ice Cream

8 Canned Vegetables / Canned Fish / Rice

9 Fresh Fruit

1. <u>Sugar</u> is in aisle __6__.

2. <u>Cookies</u> are in aisle ____.

3. <u>Ice cream</u> is in aisle ____.

4. <u>Eggs</u> are in aisle ____.

5. <u>Fruit</u> is in aisle ____.

6. Canned <u>vegetables</u> are in aisle ____.

7. <u>Napkins</u> are in aisle ____.

8. <u>Milk</u> is in aisle ____.

9. <u>Rice</u> is in aisle ____.

10. Plastic <u>bags</u> are in aisle ____.

11. <u>Potato chips</u> are in aisle ____.

12. Frozen <u>food</u> is in aisle ____.

13. <u>Bread</u> is in aisle ____.

14. Canned <u>fish</u> is in aisle ____.

15. <u>Toothbrushes</u> are in aisle ____.

EXERCISE 2: Count Nouns and Non-Count Nouns

Write the underlined words in Exercise 1 in the correct column.

Count Nouns	Non-Count Nouns
cookies	sugar
_____	_____
_____	_____
_____	_____
_____	_____
_____	_____
_____	_____
_____	_____

EXERCISE 3: Count Nouns and Non-Count Nouns; Articles

Circle the twelve words that don't belong in the lists of count nouns and non-count nouns. Two of them are already circled. Write the correct lists. Write **a, an,** or **some** before each word.

Count Nouns	Non-Count Nouns	Count Nouns	Non-Count Nouns
egg	(books)	an egg	some bread
(bread)	food	some books	some food
furniture	water	_____	_____
student	people	_____	_____
money	paper	_____	_____
information	uncle	_____	_____
teeth	homework	_____	_____
rain	advice	_____	_____
children	cell phone	_____	_____
friends	traffic	_____	_____
oil	questions	_____	_____
animal	computer	_____	_____

Complete the sentences. Circle the correct answers and write them on the lines.

1. Does the baby want _____ some milk _____ ?
   a. some milk
   b. a milk

2. The _____ for you.
   a. money isn't
   b. moneys aren't

3. There _____ in the living room.
   a. isn't any furniture
   b. aren't any furnitures

4. We don't have _____ . Hurry up!
   a. much time
   b. many times

5. Do you want _____ ?
   a. an apple
   b. some apple

6. Good. There _____ today.
   a. isn't much traffic
   b. aren't many traffics

7. Adam doesn't eat _____ .
   a. meat
   b. meats

8. Is there _____ in this store?
   a. any telephone
   b. a telephone

9. Do you have _____ ?
   a. a fruit
   b. any fruit

(continued on next page)

10. I have a lot of _____ tonight.

    a. homework

    b. homeworks

11. The students need _____.

    a. an information

    b. some information

EXERCISE 5: *A* and *The*

Complete the conversations. Use **a** *or* **the.**

  1. A: Why don't we go to ___*the*___ Chinese restaurant on Water Street?

      B: OK. I hear ___*the*___ food there is really good.

  2. A: Can I help you?

      B: Yes, I'd like _____ cup of hot chocolate, please.

  3. A: Where are your kids?

      B: They're in _____ house.

  4. A: Are you busy?

      B: Not really. I'm just looking for something on _____ Internet.

  5. A: Do you have _____ digital camera?

      B: Yes, I do, but it's pretty old.

  6. A: What is _____ name of her dog?

      B: I can't remember. It's _____ strange name.

  7. A: How was _____ party at Dan's place?

      B: It was OK. _____ music was good, and I met some new people.

  8. A: Does Paula have _____ job?

      B: Yeah. She's working as _____ receptionist at _____ publishing company.

Jack went shopping. He didn't buy everything on his shopping list, but he crossed out the things he bought. Write sentences about what he did and didn't buy. Use **some, any,** *or* **a.**

Shopping List

~~bananas~~   toothbrush

cheese   ~~potatoes~~

~~orange juice~~   lettuce

lemons   carrots

~~newspaper~~   ~~butter~~

bread   ~~milk~~

onions   ~~eggs~~

1. He bought some bananas. _____

2. He didn't buy any cheese. _____

3. _____

4. _____

5. _____

6. _____

7. _____

8. _____

9. _____

10. _____

11. _____

12. _____

13. _____

14. _____

Write true sentences. Choose words from each column.

I have	a lot of a little a few	cheese in my pocket food in my refrigerator money in my pocket books next to my bed shirts in my closet
I don't have	much many any	friends free time children work to do today questions for my teacher jewelry medicine in my bathroom problems with my English grammar photographs in my wallet ice cream at home

1. *I don't have any cheese in my pocket.*

2. _____

3. _____

4. _____

5. _____

6. _____

7. _____

8. _____

9. _____

10. _____

EXERCISE 8: Editing

Correct the conversation. There are nine mistakes. The first mistake is already corrected. Find and correct eight more.

A: How did you like ~~a~~ *the* restaurant?

B: Atmosphere was nice, but the food wasn't great. I had some fish but it didn't have

some sauce, so it was very dry. Gerry had some roast beef, but it had much salt. She

didn't eat much of it.

A: Did you have the dessert?

B: Yes, that was delicious. There were lot of choices on the menu. I had any almond

cake. Gerry had a banana ice cream with a small banana cupcake. She loved the

dessert.

A: Was the restaurant crowded?

B: There were a little people, but for a Saturday night it was pretty empty.

EXERCISE 9: Personal Writing

Write a description of one of your favorite dishes. Use both count and non-count nouns.

EXAMPLE: *I love moussaka. It's very popular in Greece. If you want to make some moussaka, you need a lot of ingredients. First of all, you need a few large potatoes, a medium eggplant, and some ground beef. You also need a few eggs, some tomatoes, and some onions. You need a few different spices, a little parsley, and some olive oil too. Moussaka has a lot of ingredients, and it takes a long time to make. But it's delicious, and a big pan of it lasts a few days.*

_____

_____

_____

_____

_____

UNIT 28 — How much / How many, Quantifiers, Enough, Adverbs of Frequency

EXERCISE 1: Containers and Non-Count Nouns

A. Match the containers and non-count nouns.

<u>b</u> **1.** a can of

2. a carton of

3. a head of

4. a loaf of

a. lettuce

b. soda

c. bread

d. milk

B. Do the same with these words.

5. a bottle of

6. a box of

7. a pack of

8. a piece of

e. cheese

f. gum

g. juice

h. cereal

C. Do the same with these words too.

9. a bar of

10. a jar of

11. a roll of

12. a tube of

i. toothpaste

j. toilet paper

k. jam

l. soap

EXERCISE 2: Questions with *How much* and *How many* and Containers

Look at Tina's cash register receipt and answer the questions.

```
6 Soda            $2.99
1 Bread           $1.95
1 Milk            $1.99
2 Lettuce         $3.98
3 Apple juice     $8.97
1 Cereal          $3.59
4 Toilet paper    $1.99
3 Soap            $2.45
1 Toothpaste      $2.50
2 Jam             $5.00

        TOTAL    $35.41
```

1. How much soda did she buy?

_____ Six cans. _____

2. How many loaves of bread did she buy?

_____ One. / One loaf. _____

3. How much milk did she buy?

_____

4. How much lettuce did she buy?

_____

5. How many bottles of apple juice did she buy?

_____

6. How many boxes of cereal did she buy?

_____

7. How much toilet paper did she buy?

_____

8. How much soap did she buy?

_____

9. How much toothpaste did she buy?

_____

10. How many jars of jam did she buy?

_____

EXERCISE 3: Questions with *How much* and *How many*

Complete the conversation. Write questions using **how much** *or* **how many**.

A: Are you going to the store?

B: Yes, why?

A: I need some things. I need some cheese.

B: _How much cheese do you need?_
　　　　　　　　　　1.

(continued on next page)

A: About a pound. And I want some eggs.

B: _How many eggs do you want?_

2.

A: A dozen. I also need some flour.

B: _____

3.

A: One pound, I think.

B: Do you want any sugar?

A: No, I have sugar.

B: _____

4.

A: I have a few cups, at least. But I want some bananas.

B: _____

5.

A: Five or six. I want some oranges too.

B: _____

6.

A: A few. Oh, and I need some cereal.

B: _____

7.

A: Just one box. I also need some potatoes.

B: _____

8.

A: Get about 10. Oh, one more thing. I want some milk.

B: _____

9.

A: Half a gallon. Oh, don't forget to get some flowers. I want roses.

B: _____

10.

A: Half a dozen.

B: Is that it? Are you sure you don't want any cookies?

A: No, I have enough cookies.

B: _____

11.

A: Two dozen. Here, let me give you some money.

B: I have money.

A: _____

12.

B: About $20.

A: Here. Take another $20.

EXERCISE 4: *Enough*

Complete the sentences. Use **is / is not enough** *and a word from the box.*

| ~~exercise~~ | fruit | sleep | spinach | television | water |

1. She exercises 60 minutes every day. That ___is enough exercise. (OR *is not enough exercise.*)___

2. The kids watch television for two hours each week. That _____

3. They eat four servings of fruit every day. That _____

4. She eats two servings of spinach every day. That _____

5. He drinks four glasses of water every day. That _____

6. They sleep six hours every day. That _____

EXERCISE 5: Adverbs of Frequency

Add an adverb of frequency to each sentence so that it is true for you. Use **always, almost always, usually, often, sometimes, almost never,** *or* **never.**

1. I drink tea in the morning.   ___I always drink tea in the morning.___

2. I bake cookies.   _____

3. I have fruit for dessert.   _____

4. I am hungry in the middle of the night.   _____

5. I drink coffee at night.   _____

6. I prepare dinner.   _____

7. I measure the ingredients when I cook.   _____

8. My food tastes good.   _____

9. My kitchen is clean.   _____

10. The stores in my neighborhood are open on Sunday.   _____

EXERCISE 6: Questions with *How often*

Write questions. Use **how often**. *Then answer the questions. Use the information in the chart.*

	Cook	Eat Out	Drink Coffee	Have Dessert
Barbara	three times a week	never	every day	rarely
Donna	once in a while	frequently	once in a while	every day
David	never	almost every day	every morning	rarely
Ed	once or twice a week	never	never	often
George	once or twice a week	almost every day	almost every day	almost never

1. (Barbara / drink coffee)

   How often does Barbara drink coffee?

   She drinks coffee every day.

2. (Donna / eat out)

3. (David / cook)

4. (Barbara and Ed / eat out)

5. (Ed / have dessert)

6. (Barbara / cook)

7. (Barbara and David / have dessert)

8. (Ed and George / cook)

_____

_____

9. (George and David / eat out)

_____

_____

10. (George / have dessert)

_____

_____

11. (Donna / have dessert

_____

_____

12. (Ed / drink coffee)

_____

_____

EXERCISE 7: Editing

Correct the conversation. There are six mistakes. The first mistake is already corrected.
Find and correct five more.

             much

A: How ~~many~~ bread pudding do you want?

B: Just a little bit. Hmm. This is delicious.

A: I don't think it has sugar enough.

B: Really? I think it's perfect. So how often you cook?

A: I cook usually every day. My wife doesn't like to cook, but I do.

B: Well, she's lucky. So how do you make this bread pudding? How many different

ingredients does it have?

A: Oh, it's pretty easy. All you need are 12 slice of bread, some eggs, some vanilla, butter,

sugar, and one cup of milk.

B: How much eggs do you need?

A: Four.

EXERCISE 8: Personal Writing

Imagine you are planning a class party. What food and drink do you need? Send an email to your classmates.

Example:

Here is what I think we need for the party:
   5 bags of potato chips
   3 bottles of soda
   12 sandwiches

EXERCISE 1: *Too*

*Complete the sentences. Use **too** and a word from the box.*

big	crowded	expensive	heavy	hot	old	~~small~~	young

1. The jeans are nice, but I wear a size 36. They're a size 34.

   They're _____*too small*_____.

2. Let's go to another restaurant. Look at all the people in this restaurant.

   It's _____.

3. The price for children under ten is five dollars. Your son can't pay five dollars. He's twelve.

   He's _____.

4. It's 38° Celsius (100.4° F) outside. I don't want to go for a walk.

   It's _____.

5. We can only take suitcases that are 20 kilos or less. Your suitcase is 40 kilos.

   It's _____.

6. I like the watch, but I never spend more than $100 on a watch. It costs $300.

   It's _____.

7. I can't wear these shoes. I wear a size 7, and they're a size 9.

   They're _____.

8. You're only fourteen years old. You can't stay at your friend's party until midnight.

   You're _____.

EXERCISE 2: *Too much*, *Too many*, and *Not enough*

Write sentences about the pictures. Use **too much**, **too many**, *or* **not enough** *and the words from the box.*

air	cars	days	furniture	~~people~~	toothpaste
birds	chairs	food	numbers	shampoo	water

1.

There are too many people

in the boat.

2. _____

_____

3. _____

_____

4. _____

_____

5. _____

_____

6. _____

_____

7. _____

_____

8. _____

_____

9. _____

_____

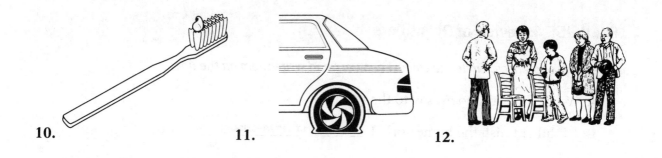

10. _____

11. _____

12. _____

_____   _____   _____

EXERCISE 3: *Too little* and *Too few*

Rewrite the sentences. Use **too little** *or* **too few.**

1. We don't have enough chairs.

We have too few chairs.

2. There isn't enough salt in this soup.

There's too little salt in this soup.

3. There weren't enough people for two teams.

_____

4. We didn't have enough paper for everyone in the class.

_____

5. There wasn't enough food for 15 people.

_____

6. You don't have enough information.

_____

7. There aren't enough bedrooms in that apartment.

_____

8. We didn't have enough time for the test.

_____

9. There aren't enough bananas for a banana cake.

_____

10. There aren't enough salesclerks at that store.

_____

Complete the sentences. Circle the correct answers and write them on the lines.

1. **A:** What did the student say to the teacher?

   B: "I didn't finish the homework. I _____*didn't have enough*_____ time."

      a. had too much

      (b.) didn't have enough

2. **A:** What did the driver say to the passenger?

   B: "We _____ gas. We need to go to the gas station."

      a. have too much

      b. don't have enough

3. **A:** What did the passenger say to the driver?

   B: "There _____ cars. Let's go to another parking lot."

      a. are too many

      b. aren't enough

4. **A:** What did the cashier say to the child?

   B: "I'm sorry. You have _____ money. Go home and get some

   more."

      a. too much

      b. too little

5. **A:** Ted and Niki wanted to see a movie, but there was a long line for tickets. What did

   Ted say?

   B: "There are _____ people. Let's see another movie."

      a. too many

      b. too few

6. **A:** What did the doctor say to the patient?

   B: "You said you're on a diet, but you lost only one pound last month. That

   _____ weight."

      a. is too much

      b. isn't enough

7. A: What did the photography teacher say to the student?

  B: "This picture is dark. You had _____ light."

  a. too much

  b. too little

8. A: What did Mitchell's mother say to him?

  B: "You ate _____ fruit. That's why you have a stomachache."

  a. too much

  b. too little

9. A: What did the customer say to the waitress?

  B: "There are _____ forks on the table for six people. Please bring some more."

  a. too many

  b. too few

10. A: What did Debbie say to her roommate?

  B: "You bought _____ juice. There's no place to put all these bottles."

  a. too much

  b. too little

EXERCISE 5: Editing

Correct the conversation. There are six mistakes. The first mistake is already corrected. Find and correct five more.

A: I can't hear you. There's too ~~many~~ *much* noise. What did you say?

B: How do you like your new neighborhood?

A: It's too much noisy. There are too much cars and too little parking places.

B: Are there places for the children to play?

A: No, there are too parks. There's only one.

B: How's the apartment?

A: It's not too small, but it costs too little money.

EXERCISE 6: Personal Writing

Imagine you do not like your home. Write what is wrong with it. Use **too many /
too much / too little** *or* **too few.** *Also use* **too** + *an adjective in your complaint.*

EXAMPLE: *I would like to move. My apartment is too small. There is too little light and too
few closets. There is only one good thing about my apartment. It is on a quiet
street, so there is not too much noise or too many cars.*

_____

_____

_____

_____

UNIT 30 Advice: *Should, Ought to, Had better*

EXERCISE 1: *Should*: Affirmative and Negative Statements

Complete the sentences. Use **should** *or* **shouldn't.**

1. Children ____shouldn't____ play with matches.

2. Children _____ watch television all day long.

3. Children _____ listen to their parents.

4. Children _____ eat a lot of candy.

5. Children _____ play in the street.

6. Teenagers _____ pay attention in school.

7. Teenagers _____ keep their bedrooms neat.

8. Teenagers _____ stay out all night with their friends.

9. Adults _____ exercise at least twice a week.

10. Adults _____ drink 10 cups of coffee a day.

EXERCISE 2: *Ought to*: Affirmative Statements

Rewrite the sentences. Use **ought to.**

1. You should read this book about cultural differences.

    You ought to read this book about cultural differences.
    _____

2. I should look up information about the country on the Internet.

    _____

    _____

3. Business people should learn about the customs of other countries.

    _____

    _____

(continued on next page)

179

4. The visitor should bring a gift.

_____

5. We should be careful.

_____

6. To avoid confusion, you should always put the date on your paperwork.

_____

EXERCISE 3: _Should_: Affirmative Statements

Rewrite the sentences. Use **should.**

1. We ought to ask if it's OK.

We should ask if it's OK.

2. I ought to learn how to speak the language.

_____

3. Ms. Jones ought to put her email address on her business card.

_____

4. You ought to plan your trip carefully.

_____

5. The students ought to ask more questions.

_____

6. We ought to avoid making that gesture; people consider it an insult.

_____

EXERCISE 4: _Should_: Affirmative and Negative Statements

Complete the sentences. Use **should** _or_ **shouldn't** _and the words from the box._

go to the dentist	look for another one	study more	wash it
leave a tip	~~see a doctor~~	touch it	watch it
leave early	smoke		

1. Dave is sick. He _should see a doctor._

2. I don't like my job. I _____

3. John often has a bad cough. He _____

4. Myra has a toothache. She _____

5. The car is dirty. We _____

6. The waiter is terrible. We _____

7. Doug and Jason aren't doing well in math. They _____

8. There's going to be a lot of traffic. We _____

9. That movie is very violent. The children _____

10. That dog may bite. You _____

EXERCISE 5: *Should*: *Wh-* Questions

Complete the conversation. Write questions with **should.** *Use* **who, what, when, where, why,** *or* **how many** *and the verbs in parentheses.*

A: Let's have a party.

B: OK. _____ When should we have _____ it?
                            1. (have)

A: Let's have it on March 23rd.

B: _____ it then?
                   2. (have)

A: Because it's Lucy's birthday.

B: Oh, that's right. _____?
                            3. (invite)

A: Probably around 25 people.

B: _____?
              4. (invite)

A: Let's see . . . the neighbors, Lucy's family, and the people from the office.

B: _____?
              5. (buy)

A: Well, we'll need drinks, potato chips, and things like that.

B: _____?
              6. (cook)

A: I'll make some lasagna.

B: That sounds good. I'll make some salad. _____
                                                          7. (get)

a birthday cake?

A: I like the Savoy Bakery's cakes.

B: OK. Let's order one from there.

(continued on next page)

A: You know, we don't have enough dishes and glasses for 25 people.

_____?
8. (do)

B: That's no problem. We can get paper plates and cups at the supermarket.

A: You're right. That's a good idea. _____ out the
9. (send)

invitations?

B: I'll write them this weekend.

EXERCISE 6: *Had better*: Affirmative and Negative Statements

Match the situations with the advice. Each piece of advice will be used twice.

__c__ **1.** We'd better take a taxi.	**a.** We're lost.
____ **2.** We'd better ask for directions.	**b.** We're getting red.
____ **3.** We'd better not stay up late.	**c.** We're going to be late.
____ **4.** We'd better make sure everything is locked.	**d.** We'll be away for three weeks.
____ **5.** We'd better look at a map.	**e.** We have an exam tomorrow.
____ **6.** We'd better not wait for the bus.	
____ **7.** We'd better not stay in the sun anymore.	
____ **8.** We'd better get a good night's sleep.	
____ **9.** We'd better throw away the food in the refrigerator.	
____ **10.** We'd better put some sunblock on our arms and legs.	

EXERCISE 7: *Had better*: Affirmative and Negative Statements

Don and Amy are planning a dinner party. Complete the conversation. Use **had better** *or*
had better not *and the words from the box.*

ask Costas to bring her	invite him	~~serve roast beef~~
borrow some from the neighbors	let the dog in the house	serve shrimp
get a couple of bottles	rent a video	sit together at the table

DON: What kind of food should we serve? How about roast beef?

AMY: Alan can't eat beef.

DON: Well, then we _____ *had better not serve roast beef* _____. How about shrimp?
1.

AMY: Joan doesn't like fish or seafood.

DON: Then we _____. How about chicken?
2.

AMY: Good idea. Do we have enough drinks?

DON: Ed drinks only Diet Coke. We _____.

  Is Chris coming? She's allergic to animals. We _____.

AMY: How is Sandy getting here? She doesn't drive and lives far from here.

DON: We _____.

AMY: What do you think of the seating plan?

DON: Marsha and Sophia _____. They don't

  like each other.

AMY: I just remembered Tonya has a new boyfriend. We

  _____. And Ted and Marsha are bringing

  their children.

DON: They will probably get bored. We _____.

AMY: How many guests are coming? We won't have enough chairs.

DON: We _____.

EXERCISE 8: Editing

Correct the conversation. There are six mistakes. The first mistake is already corrected.
Find and correct five more.

        had

A: You ~~have~~ better not wear that to the reception. You should to wear something

  more formal.

B: Should I wearing this?

A: Yeah. I think that's better. And you ought to wear a tie.

B: Really? Then I better had change my shoes. Ought I to wear these brown ones?

A: No, I think the black ones are better.

B: What time I should leave?

A: Soon. You don't want to be late.

EXERCISE 9: Personal Writing

Write advice for dinner guests. Use **should** *and* **shouldn't.**

EXAMPLE: When you go to someone's home for dinner, you should bring a gift. Some chocolates or flowers are always a nice gift. You shouldn't arrive early and you shouldn't arrive more than a few minutes late. If you're going to be late, you should call. At the table, you shouldn't serve yourself. You should wait for your host or hostess to serve you. Finally, you should say the food is good, even if it isn't!

_____

_____

_____

_____

Requests, Desires, and Offers: *Would you, Could you, Can you . . . ?, I'd like . . .*

Read each conversation. Then answer the question.

Conversation A

A: Can I help you?

B: Yes, I'd like two tickets to Pittsburgh.

A: Would you like one-way or round-trip?

B: Round-trip, please.

A: That's $70.

B: Here you are. What time is the next bus?

A: At 9:30.

B: Thank you.

1. Where does Conversation A take place? _____

Conversation B

A: Sir, would you like chicken or fish?

B: Chicken, please.

A: And what would you like to drink?

B: Just some water, please.

A: And your wife?

B: She doesn't want anything. She doesn't like airplane food.

2. Where does Conversation B take place? _____

(continued on next page)

Conversation C

A: Where would you like to sit?

B: These seats are fine. I don't want to sit too close to the screen.

A: Would you like some popcorn?

B: No, but I'd like something to drink. But hurry! The movie's going to start.

3. Where does Conversation C take place? _____

EXERCISE 2: *Would like*: Affirmative Statements and *Yes / No* Questions

Rewrite the sentences. Use **would like.**

1. I want two tickets for *Heartless,* please.

   I would like two tickets for "Heartless," please.

2. Do you want to go to the movies tonight?

   Would you like to go to the movies tonight?

3. The teacher wants to see you.

   _____

4. Do the children want hamburgers or hot dogs?

   _____

5. Do you want to check your email on my computer?

   _____

6. Does Paul want to come to the party?

   _____

7. My husband wants rice with his fish.

   _____

8. Neil and Jane want a bigger apartment.

   _____

9. Do you want to have a cup of coffee with me?

   _____

10. We want to go home now.

   _____

EXERCISE 3: *Would like*: Statements and Questions

Complete the conversation. Use the words in parentheses.

DAVE: Hi, Ellen. Come on in.

ELLEN: Hi, Dave. Thanks.

DAVE: _____ *Would you like* _____ some coffee?
    1. (you / like)

ELLEN: Yes. That sounds good. _____ some help?
    2. (you / like)

DAVE: No, it's ready. Here you are.

ELLEN: Thanks.

DAVE: _____ some cookies too?
    3. (you / like)

ELLEN: No, thanks, but I _____ some sugar for my
    4. (like)

coffee.

DAVE: Oh, sorry. I forgot. Here's the sugar.

ELLEN: Boy, it's cold outside.

DAVE: _____ a sweater?
    5. (you / like)

ELLEN: No, I'm OK.

DAVE: So, _____ this evening?
    6. (what / you / like / do)

ELLEN: I don't know. _____?
    7. (Where / you / like / go)

DAVE: _____ to the movies?
    8. (you / like / go)

ELLEN: What's playing?

DAVE: *Forever Love* is at the Rex. _____ that?
    9. (you / like / see)

ELLEN: OK. What time does it start?

DAVE: We can go at six, eight, or ten.

ELLEN: I don't care. _____?
    10. (What time / you / like / go)

DAVE: Eight is fine, but I _____ something to eat first.
    11. (like / get)

ELLEN: OK. _____?
    12. (Where / you / like / eat)

DAVE: How about John's Pizzeria?

ELLEN: That sounds good.

Write correct questions. Use **please** *with* **would you, could you,** *or* **can you.**

1. Ask a stranger on the bus to tell you the time.

   Would you please tell me the time? OR *Could you please tell me the time?*
   _____

2. Ask a desk clerk at a hotel to give you the key to your room.

   _____

3. Ask your teacher to explain the meaning of the word *selfish*.

   _____

4. Ask a cashier to give you change for a dollar.

   _____

5. Ask a stranger to take a picture of you and your friends.

   _____

6. Ask a taxi driver to take you to the airport.

   _____

7. Ask a neighbor to lend you a hand with your suitcases.

   _____

8. Ask a salesclerk to show you the brown shoes in the window.

   _____

9. Ask the person in front of you at a basketball game to sit down.

   _____

EXERCISE 5: Responses

Complete the conversations. Circle the correct answers and write them on the lines.

1. **A:** Would you like some cream in your coffee?

   B: _No, thank you._
   _____

   a. No, I wouldn't.

   (b.) No, thank you.

2. A: Would you like to have dinner with us tonight?

B: _____

    a. Yes, I would. Thank you.

    b. I do.

3. A: Could you move your bag, please?

B: _____

    a. Sure.

    b. I could.

4. A: Would you help me?

B: _____

    a. Yes, thanks.

    b. Of course.

5. A: Can you give me a lift to the office?

B: _____

    a. I'm sorry, I can't. My car's not working.

    b. No, I don't.

6. A: Would you like something to drink?

B: _____

    a. Yes, I would. Thanks.

    b. Yes, I would like.

EXERCISE 6: Editing

Correct the conversation. There are six mistakes. The first mistake is already corrected.
Find and correct five more.

    Would
A: ~~Do~~ you like some help?

B: Yes, thank you. Could you to lend me a hand with these boxes?

A: Yes, I could. So how would you like the building?

B: I like it a lot, but I like to meet the neighbors. I don't know many people yet.

A: Would you like to come to my party tonight? A lot of the neighbors will be there.

(continued on next page)

Requests, Desires, and Offers: *Would you, Could you, Can you . . . ?, I'd like . . .*   **189**

B: That sounds great . . . Well, I think that's all the boxes. Would you like some coffee?

A: No, I wouldn't like any, thank you. See you tonight at 8. Apartment 3F.

EXERCISE 7: Personal Writing

Imagine one of your neighbors emails you a request. Write the email. Then write your response.

EXAMPLE:

Hi, Deb,

Sam and I are going on vacation on Monday. We'll be away for two weeks. Would you please take in our newspapers?

Thanks so much!

Carol

Hi, Carol,

Sure, I'd be glad to take in your newspapers for you.

I hope you have a wonderful vacation!

Deb

Necessity: *Have to, Don't have to, Must, Mustn't*

Put a check (✓) next to the sentences that are true.

____ **1.** People in my country have to pay taxes.

____ **2.** People in my country don't have to vote.

____ **3.** Drivers in my country have to have driver's licenses.

____ **4.** Students in my country don't have to wear uniforms in high school.

____ **5.** Young people in my country don't have to do military service.

____ **6.** Women in my country had to obey their husbands 50 years ago.

____ **7.** Children in my country did not have to go to school 50 years ago.

____ **8.** Children in my country had to go to work at a young age 50 years ago.

EXERCISE 2: *Have to*: Affirmative and Negative Statements

Complete the sentences. Use **have to** *and* **don't have to** *in each sentence.*

1. Students _____*don't have to*_____ stay in school 12 hours a day, but they

_____*have to*_____ pass their exams.

2. Teachers _____ correct papers, but they

_____ wear uniforms.

3. Police officers _____ speak a foreign language, but they

_____ wear uniforms.

4. Doctors _____ study for many years, but they

_____ know how to type.

5. Secretaries _____ work at night, but they

_____ know how to type.

6. Firefighters _____ work at night, but they

_____ study for many years.

(continued on next page)

7. Fashion models _____ work seven days a week, but they

_____ worry about their appearance.

8. Farmers _____ get up early in the morning, but they

_____ worry about their appearance.

9. Basketball players _____ practice regularly, but they

_____ play a game every day.

10. Accountants _____ be good writers, but they

_____ be good with numbers.

EXERCISE 3: *Have to*: Affirmative and Negative Statements

Complete the conversations. Use **have to, has to, don't have to,** *or* **doesn't have to.**

1. **A:** Is Dan getting up early this morning?

   B: No, he _____ *doesn't have to get up early this morning* _____. There's no school.

2. **A:** Is Sheila leaving early today?

   B: Yes, she _____. She has an appointment

   with her dentist.

3. **A:** Are you going food shopping today?

   B: Yes, I _____. There's no food in the house.

4. **A:** Are you and your wife taking a taxi?

   B: Yes, we _____. Our car isn't working.

5. **A:** Is Barbara working late today?

   B: No, she _____. Her boss is on vacation.

6. **A:** Are the children cleaning up their room?

   B: No, they _____. I cleaned it up yesterday.

7. **A:** Is Mary taking some medicine?

   B: Yes, she _____. She has a stomach

   problem.

8. **A:** Are you paying for the tickets?

   B: No, we _____. They're free.

9. **A:** Is José wearing a suit and tie this morning?

   B: Yes, he _____. He has an important

   business meeting.

10. **A:** Does Bonnie do housework?

    B: No, she _____. She has a maid.

EXERCISE 4: *Have to*: Present and Past Affirmative and Negative Statements

Rewrite the sentences. Use **have to, has to, don't have to, doesn't have to, had to,** *or* **didn't have to.**

1. It's necessary for me to finish this exercise.

   I have to finish this exercise.

2. It isn't necessary for me to write everything 10 times.

   _____

3. It wasn't necessary for the teacher to come early yesterday.

   _____

4. It was necessary for one student to stay after class yesterday.

   _____

5. It isn't necessary for me to check my email every day.

   _____

6. It wasn't necessary for my friends to work last week.

   _____

7. It's necessary for the school to have clean classrooms.

   _____

8. It isn't necessary for the teacher to work on the weekend.

   _____

9. It's necessary for students to have a 75 percent average to pass that course.

   _____

10. It's necessary for me to write down the new words.

    _____

What does each sign mean? Write sentences. Use **must** *or* **mustn't** *and the words from the box.*

drive faster than 55 mph	make a U-turn	stop
~~enter~~	park in this area	turn left
go more slowly	pass	turn right

DO NOT [ ] ENTER

1.

STOP

2.

3.

4.

SPEED LIMIT 55

5.

NO PARKING ANY TIME

6.

7.

8.

MEN AT WORK

9.

1. _You mustn't enter._ _____

2. _____

3. _____

4. _____

5. _____

6. _____

7. _____

8. _____

9. _____

EXERCISE 6: *Had to*: Affirmative and Negative Statements

Mr. and Mrs. Chung were on vacation last week. Write sentences. Use **had to** *or*
didn't have to *and the words from the box.*

~~do any work~~	look for a hotel
find someone to take care of their dog	make the bed every morning
get to the airport on time	pack and unpack suitcases
get up early every morning	pay their hotel bill
go to work	wash dishes

1. *They didn't have to do any work.*

2. _____

3. _____

4. _____

5. _____

6. _____

7. _____

8. _____

9. _____

10. _____

EXERCISE 7: *Have to*: Past and Present *Yes / No* Questions and Short Answers

Put the words in the correct order. Write questions with **have to***. Then answer the*
questions. Use short answers.

1. have to / English / in class / you / Do / speak

    Do you have to speak English in class?

    Yes, we do. OR *No, we don't.*

2. get up / your / have to / Does / in the morning / at six o'clock / mother

    _____

    _____

    (continued on next page)

3. you / last night / cook / Did / have to

_____

_____

4. best friend / do / Does / have to / your / this exercise

_____

_____

5. you / on time / in / have to / English class / Do / be

_____

_____

6. friends / learn / Do / English / your / have to

_____

_____

7. shave / father / have to / your / Did / yesterday

_____

_____

8. your / to work / best friend / yesterday / Did / have to / go

_____

_____

9. a / test / you / have to / Did / last week / take

_____

_____

EXERCISE 8: *Have to*: Past and Present *Wh-* Questions

Write questions. Use **have to.**

1. I have to see someone.

Who *do you have to see?* _____

2. She has to take a test.

When _____

3. He has to leave early.

Why _____

4. The students had to wait for their teacher.

How long _____

5. We had to meet after class.

Why _____

6. The teacher has to talk to the parents of some students.

How many parents _____

7. He had to pay a lot for the class.

How much _____

8. She has to buy a lot of books.

How many books _____

9. I have to finish my paper.

When _____

10. The schools had to close.

What time _____

EXERCISE 9: Editing

Correct the conversation. There are six mistakes. The first mistake is already corrected.
Find and correct five more.

A: You mustn't ⨉ talk to your neighbor during the exam. You have to be quiet and have

to work fast. You have only one hour for the exam.

B: Excuse me? Have we to use a pencil?

A: No, you don't have. You can use a pencil or a pen.

C: Excuse me? Can I use my electronic dictionary during the exam?

A: No, you have put everything away. You don't have to have anything on your desks

except the exam. Any more questions? OK. We must get started.

EXERCISE 10: Personal Writing

Write about the rules in your English class. Use **have to, must,** *and* **mustn't.**

EXAMPLE: *In my English class we have to speak English all the time. We mustn't speak our own language. We also have to be on time for class, and we have to do all the assignments. We don't have to take a midterm or final exam, but we have to do two oral presentations. In fact, I must give my second presentation next week. I'd better write an outline for it now.*

_____

_____

_____

_____

UNIT 33 The Comparative

EXERCISE 1: Comparative Form of Adjectives

Put a check (✓) next to the statements that are true.

- ✓ **1.** New York has a bigger population than Boston.
- _____ **2.** Los Angeles is farther from New York than Chicago is.
- _____ **3.** Boston has warmer winters than Miami.
- _____ **4.** San Francisco is an older city than New York.
- _____ **5.** Los Angeles has milder winters than Chicago.
- _____ **6.** Libraries are noisier than nightclubs.
- _____ **7.** Cell phones are more expensive than computers.
- _____ **8.** Trains are faster than planes.
- _____ **9.** Adults are younger than children.
- _____ **10.** Driving is more dangerous than walking.

EXERCISE 2: Comparative Form of Adjectives

Put the words from the box in the correct columns.

~~big~~	dangerous	fast	hot	noisy
~~careful~~	diverse	friendly	intelligent	old
~~comfortable~~	easy	heavy	long	pretty
crowded	expensive	high	messy	small

One Syllable	Two Syllables	Three or Four Syllables
big	careful	comfortable

EXERCISE 3: Comparative Form of Adjectives

Complete the sentences. Use the comparative form of the adjectives.

1. That city is old, but this city is _____older_____.

2. That port is beautiful, but this port is _____.

3. The climate in Baltimore is mild, but the climate in Miami is _____.

4. Boston is big, but Chicago is _____.

5. That neighborhood is diverse, but this neighborhood is _____.

6. The train station is far, but the airport is _____.

7. Tom is intelligent, but his brother is _____.

8. The service at that restaurant is bad, but the food is _____.

9. My sister is messy, but my brother is _____.

10. This chair is comfortable, but that chair is _____.

11. My husband is careful, but his father is _____.

12. This picture is pretty, but that picture is _____.

13. Chemistry is difficult, but physics is _____.

14. This exercise is easy, but the last exercise was _____.

15. That book is good, but this book is _____.

EXERCISE 4: Comparative Form of Adjectives

Complete the sentences with the correct adjectives. Use the comparative form of the adjectives in parentheses and **than.**

1. San Francisco is _____smaller than_____ New York.

(big / small)

2. The Nile River is _____ the Mississippi River.

(long / short)

3. A Mercedes is _____ a Volkswagen.

(cheap / expensive)

4. An ocean is _____ a lake.

(big / small)

5. Mountains are _____ hills.

(low / high)

6. Egypt is _____ Canada.

(cold / hot)

7. Skiing is _____ golf.
   (safe / dangerous)

8. Cities are _____ villages.
   (crowded / empty)

9. Cars are _____ bicycles.
   (noisy / quiet)

10. A rock is _____ a leaf.
   (heavy / light)

11. Rabbits are _____ snails.
   (slow / fast)

12. Dogs are _____ wolves.
   (friendly / unfriendly)

EXERCISE 5: Comparative Form of Adjectives

Write questions. Use the comparative form of the adjectives. Then answer the questions.

1. your mother / old / or / young / your father

   Is your mother older or younger than your father?   She is younger. OR She's older.

2. which / difficult / English / your language

   Which is more difficult, English or your language?   English.

3. this book / cheap / or / expensive / your notebook

   _____   _____

4. your country / big / or / small / Canada

   _____   _____

5. your English pronunciation / good / or / bad / last year

   _____   _____

6. which / healthy / coffee / tea

   _____   _____

7. which / nice / dinner at home / dinner in a restaurant

   _____   _____

EXERCISE 6: Editing

Correct the conversation. There are six mistakes. The first mistake is already corrected.
Find and correct five more.

A: I'm thinking about moving to Brighton. Apartments there are ~~more~~ cheaper.

B: Brighton will be less convenient. It is more far from your job.

A: Yeah, but not a lot. I can take the highway, so my commute won't be much long.

B: The highway is busier from the small streets you use now.

A: But there are no traffic lights on the highway. Besides, I don't go to work until 10 A.M.

The traffic is badder from 7 to 9.

B: Well, I hope you find a nice place. It's probably more easy to find something now.

EXERCISE 7: Personal Writing

Compare the place where you live with a place you would like to visit. Use at least three comparative adjectives.

EXAMPLE: *I live in Valence in France. I would really like to visit New York. New York is much bigger and much more crowded than Valence. That's why I'm sure Valence is quieter than New York. Valence isn't a very exciting town, especially at night. New York is probably a lot more exciting. It certainly looks much more exciting in the movies.*

_____

_____

_____

_____

UNIT 34 Adverbs of Manner

EXERCISE 1: Adjectives vs. Adverbs

*Write **adjective** if the underlined word is an adjective. Write **adverb** if it is an adverb.*

1. She speaks <u>clearly</u>. _____ *adverb* _____

2. The speaker told several <u>bad</u> jokes. _____ *adjective* _____

3. He gave a <u>lively</u> presentation. _____

4. The car is <u>dirty</u>. _____

5. Cab drivers should drive <u>carefully</u>. _____

6. This exercise isn't <u>hard</u>. _____

7. My husband always gets up <u>early</u>. _____

8. I don't want to do <u>badly</u> on the test. _____

9. That girl runs <u>fast</u>. _____

10. That jacket looks <u>good</u> on you. _____

11. Those shoes are <u>ugly</u>. _____

12. I want to speak English <u>fluently</u>. _____

13. Talk <u>slowly</u>. _____

14. He is <u>polite</u>. _____

15. They work <u>hard</u>. _____

EXERCISE 2: Adverbs of Manner

Circle the ten adverbs in the box.

B	H	A	P	P	I	L	Y	F	A	X	M
A	E	A	S	I	L	Y	Q	A	X	D	O
D	A	N	G	E	R	O	U	S	L	Y	S
L	V	G	X	X	C	X	I	T	E	X	X
Y	I	R	P	A	T	I	E	N	T	L	Y
X	L	I	A	F	X	X	T	O	C	X	D
E	Y	L	S	W	E	L	L	B	N	O	R
X	X	Y	N	X	N	L	Y	I	K	X	E

EXERCISE 3: Adverbs of Manner

Complete the sentences. Use the adverbs in Exercise 2.

1. It's snowing _____*heavily*_____. We can't drive in this weather.

2. Please talk _____. The baby's sleeping.

3. Vinny drives _____. One day he's going to have an accident.

4. Lenore was an hour late for class. Her teacher looked at her _____.

5. The children played with their toys _____.

6. She plays the guitar very _____. Everyone loves to listen to her.

7. I never eat my father's food. He cooks _____.

8. I can't understand him. He speaks _____.

9. I waited _____, but the doctor never came.

10. Your directions were very good. I found the restaurant _____.

EXERCISE 4: Adjectives and Adverbs

Complete the conversations. Use the adjectives from the box or their adverb forms.

angry	careful	fast	~~quiet~~	tired
bad	easy	good	serious	

1. A: Shh! Be _____quiet_____! This is a library.

   B: Talk _____quietly_____.

2. A: The potatoes taste _____.

   B: Yes, they are very _____. I'll have some more.

3. A: Is Nicole a _____ runner?

   B: Yes, she runs very _____. She wins races all the time.

4. A: Go to bed. You look _____.

   B: But I'm not _____.

5. A: Is Martha _____ with her boyfriend?

   B: I think so. Yesterday, she spoke to him _____, and now she's not

     talking to him.

6. A: Is Kim a _____ typist?

   B: Yes, she types _____. She never makes mistakes.

7. A: Was the test _____?

   B: Yes, I answered all the questions _____. I didn't have any problems

     at all.

8. A: Why are you so unhappy? Was the game _____?

   B: Yes, it was. We lost. Everybody played _____.

9. A: Kevin's always so _____. He hardly ever smiles.

   B: I know. He does everything so _____.

EXERCISE 5: Editing

Correct the conversation. There are six mistakes. The first mistake is already corrected.
Find and correct five more.

> **A:** How was the food at the reception? Did it taste ~~well~~ *good*?
>
> **B:** Yeah, it was pretty good. But the service was badly. And after the meal, we had to
>
> listen to two more speeches. The first speaker spoke very fastly, and the second spoke
>
> very slowly.
>
> **A:** Were they interesting speeches?
>
> **B:** Not really. The speakers didn't know their audience good. The topics of the speeches
>
> sounded good, but the speeches were boringly. And I was tired, so I didn't listen very
>
> careful.

EXERCISE 6: Personal Writing

Write advice for someone who wants to learn something new. Use three adverbs
of manner.

> **EXAMPLE:** It's difficult to learn a new language but if you study hard, you can do it. You have
> to study the grammar carefully, and you have to learn some new words every day.
> I think six to eight is a good number. Finally, you have to practice speaking a lot.
> That's how you will learn to speak the language fluently.

_____

_____

_____

_____

EXERCISE 1: *Too* and *Enough*

Match the questions and answers.

  _c_   **1.** Do you want to go to the movies with us?   **a.** No, it's too cold.

_____ **2.** Can I go to the party tonight?   **b.** No, it's too expensive.

_____ **3.** Why are you looking for a new apartment?   **c.** No, it's too late.

_____ **4.** Are you going to the beach today?   **d.** No, he's too fussy.

_____ **5.** Are you going to buy the necklace?   **e.** He's not serious enough.

_____ **6.** Is your son on the swim team?   **f.** No, he's not fast enough.

_____ **7.** Why doesn't Joe do well in school?   **g.** Ours isn't big enough.

_____ **8.** Do you like to cook for Adam?   **h.** No, you're not old enough.

EXERCISE 2: *Too* + Adjective

Rewrite the sentences. Use **too** *and change the adjective.*

1. The box isn't light enough to carry.

    The box is too heavy to carry.

2. The questions aren't easy enough to answer.

_____

3. The shirt isn't big enough to wear.

_____

4. It isn't cool enough outside to go running.

_____

5. The store isn't close enough to walk.

_____

6. The soup isn't hot enough to eat.

_____

EXERCISE 3: Adjective + *Not enough*

Rewrite the sentences. Use **not enough** *and change the adjective.*

1. It's too noisy in here to talk.

   It's not quiet enough in here to talk.

2. The story was too boring.

   _____

3. Your room is too messy.

   _____

4. Your hair is too long.

   _____

5. You're too young to watch that kind of TV program.

   _____

6. The numbers are too small to see.

   _____

EXERCISE 4: *Too* and *Very*

Complete the sentences. Use **too** *or* **very**.

1. A: Do you like my new shirt?

   B: Yes, it's _____ *very* _____ nice.

2. A: Put these sweaters in the drawer.

   B: I can't. The drawer's _____ full.

3. A: Mommy, I want to swim in the baby pool.

   B: You're _____ big. You're not a baby.

4. A: What do you think of that hotel?

   B: The rooms are _____ nice, but it's _____ expensive.

5. A: How's the weather in Montreal in January?

   B: It's _____ cold.

6. **A:** Can you read that sign?

   B: No, it's _____ far away.

7. **A:** Are you going to buy the stereo?

   B: I think so. The price is _____ good.

8. **A:** The floor's _____ dirty.

   B: I'll wash it.

9. **A:** Put this bag in your pocket.

   B: I can't. It's _____ big.

EXERCISE 5: *Too* or *Enough* + Adjective + Infinitive

Combine the sentences. Use **too** *or* **enough** *and an infinitive.*

1. You can't marry Robert. He's too old.

   Robert's too old to marry. _____

2. You can't buy that cell phone. It's too expensive.

   _____

3. I can't wait. I'm too tired.

   _____

4. Sandra didn't eat the steak. It was too tough.

   _____

5. Jeffrey can't drive. He isn't old enough.

   _____

6. They can't play on the team. They aren't good enough.

   _____

7. I can't drink the tea. It's too hot.

   _____

8. She can do the work. She's smart enough.

   _____

Complete the conversations. Use **too, enough,** *or* **not enough** *and the adjective in parentheses.*

1. **A:** Why did you take the pants back to the store?

    B: They were _____ too long _____. I exchanged them for a shorter pair.
    (long)

2. **A:** Do you want me to wash the car again?

    B: Yes. It's _____ not clean enough _____.
    (clean)

3. **A:** Let's go into that big old house. I want to see what's in there.

    B: No, I'm _____. There may be ghosts.
    (frightened)

4. **A:** Are the shoes comfortable?

    B: No, they're _____. I need a size 8, and they're a size 7.
    (big)

5. **A:** Why didn't you get the tickets?

    B: It was _____. There weren't any left.
    (late)

6. **A:** Is the soup _____?
    (hot)

    B: Yeah. Thanks for heating it up.

7. **A:** How are the pants?

    B: They're _____. I think I need a larger size.
    (tight)

8. **A:** Why do I need to rewrite this composition?

    B: Because it's _____. It's only 150 words, and I told you to
    (short)
    write at least 250 words.

9. **A:** Can I borrow your bike?

    B: No, there's something wrong with the brakes. It's _____
    (safe)
    to ride.

10. **A:** Dad, can we go in the water now?

    B: I don't know. It was cold before. Put your toe in the water and see if it's

    _____ now.
    (warm)

11. **A:** Why aren't the plants in the living room growing?

    B: Probably because it's _____. They need more light.
    (sunny)

Put a check (✓) next to the statements that are true.

_____ **1.** China is the same size as France.

___✓___ **2.** Lions are not as big as elephants.

_____ **3.** 32° F is the same temperature as 0° C.

_____ **4.** The Statue of Liberty in New York is not as old as the Pyramids in Egypt.

_____ **5.** Canada is as cold as Antarctica.

_____ **6.** A whale is different from a fish.

_____ **7.** An orange is the same color as a carrot.

_____ **8.** Silver is as valuable as gold.

EXERCISE 8: *Than* **and** *As*

Complete the sentences. Use **as** *or* **than.**

1. Russia is bigger ___than___ the United States.

2. Is your classroom the same size ___as___ the other classrooms?

3. South America is not as big _____ Asia.

4. English is more difficult _____ my native language.

5. My mother is not the same age _____ my father.

6. I'm more tired today _____ I was yesterday.

7. Are doctors as rich _____ lawyers?

8. Is she as thin _____ her mother?

9. Thelma's the same height _____ her brother.

10. Are animals more intelligent _____ human beings?

11. This book is better _____ that one.

12. Some people are more difficult _____ others.

Write sentences. Use the adjective in parentheses and **as . . . as, not as . . . as,** *or* **more . . . than.** *(Remember:* = *means* **equals,** < *means* **less than,** > *means* **more than.***)*

1. a Hyundai < a Mercedes (expensive)

   A Hyundai isn't as expensive as a Mercedes.

2. the book > the film (interesting)

   The book is more interesting than the film.

3. my apartment = your apartment (big)

   My apartment is as big as your apartment.

4. trains < airplanes (fast)

   _____

5. January = February (cold)

   _____

6. the chair = the sofa (comfortable)

   _____

7. the governor of Oregon < the president of the United States (famous)

   _____

8. the bank < the post office (far)

   _____

9. limes = lemons (sour)

   _____

10. jazz > rock music (relaxing)

    _____

11. chocolate ice cream < vanilla ice cream (good)

    _____

12. some people > other people (violent)

    _____

13. college < high school (easy)

_____

14. these boxes = those boxes (heavy)

_____

EXERCISE 10: *The same* + Noun + *As*

*Write questions. Use **the same . . . as** and a noun from the box.*

age	~~color~~	distance	height	length	price	size	weight

1. *Is your sister's hair the same color as your hair?* _____

No. My sister's hair is brown. My hair's black.

2. _____

No. I'm 1.69 meters tall. My brother's 1.78 meters tall.

3. _____

No. My mother's 59 years old. My father's 62.

4. _____

No. The dining room's smaller than the living room.

5. _____

Yes. The apples and the pears are both 90¢ a pound.

6. _____

No. I'm thinner than my brother.

7. _____

No. *War and Peace* is much longer than *Crime and Punishment*.

8. _____

No. The subway station is farther than the bus stop.

Write sentences. Use **the same as** *or* **different from.**

1. a niece and a nephew

   A niece is different from a nephew.

2. the U.S.A. and the United States

   The U.S.A. is the same as the United States.

3. a bike and a bicycle

4. a TV and a television

5. North America and the United States

6. 10,362 and 10.362

7. 3×16 and 16×3

8. $16 \div 3$ and $3 \div 16$

9. $1 and £1

10. a snack bar and a restaurant

11. 12:00 P.M. and noon

12. a plane and an airplane

EXERCISE 12: Editing

Correct the conversation. There are eight mistakes. The first mistake is already corrected.
Find and correct seven more.

                                          big enough

A: That black jacket isn't ~~enough big~~.

B: Really? It feels comfortable enough.

A: It doesn't look good on you. How about this green jacket? It is the same price from that one.

B: But it isn't warm as this black jacket. I want something that is too warm.

A: There are some other jackets over there. They don't look very different than the black one.

B: Hmm . . . This one is as nicer as the black one, but it doesn't have pockets enough.

A: So you want a warm jacket with lots of pockets.

B: Exactly. And one that isn't too small for me wear.

EXERCISE 13: Personal Writing

Write an email in which you explain why you want to return an item. Use **enough, too /**
very, the same *(+ noun)* **as, different from,** *and* **as + adjective + as.**

    EXAMPLE:

> I want to return this jacket because it isn't large enough. Also, it is too formal, and the color isn't very nice. The jacket looks different from the picture on the website. The quality is not as good as usual.

36 The Superlative

EXERCISE 1: The Superlative

Look at the restaurant reviews and answer the questions.

	Donnelly's	The Big Oven	Circo	Shanghai Garden
Prices	$$$$	$$	$$$	$
Quality of Food	7.5	9.5	7	10
Friendliness of Staff	7.5	10	8	7.5
Cleanliness	10	9	7	9.5
Atmosphere	9	9.5	10	7
Size	35 tables	20 tables	60 tables	35 tables
Overall Rating	**8.5**	**9.5**	**8**	**8.5**

Which restaurant . . . ?

1. is the most expensive? _____Donnelly's_____

2. has the most delicious food? _____

3. has the friendliest staff? _____

4. is the cleanest? _____

5. is the biggest? _____

6. has the nicest atmosphere? _____

7. is the best? _____

EXERCISE 2: The Superlative Form of Adjectives

Complete the sentences. Use the superlative form of the adjective.

1. The kitchen is always hot. It's _____the hottest_____ room in the house.

2. Roger's a bad student. He's _____ student in the class.

3. Chemistry is hard. For me, it's _____ subject in school.

4. Roses are beautiful. I think that roses are _____ flowers.

5. Noon is a busy time at the bank. In fact, it's _____ time.

6. *Married Young* is a funny program. It's _____ program on TV.

7. Scully's is a good restaurant. In fact, it's _____ restaurant in town.

8. Monkeys are ugly. In my opinion, they're _____ animals in the zoo.

9. Midnight is a popular nightclub. It's _____ nightclub in town.

10. Dixon's has low prices. It has _____ prices in the neighborhood.

11. Pamela's a fast swimmer. She's _____ swimmer on the team.

12. Jake is charming. He's _____ of all my friends.

EXERCISE 3: The Superlative and *One of the*

Write questions with **one of the** *and the superlative form of the adjective. Then answer the questions.*

1. What / long / rivers in the world?

   What is one of the longest rivers in the world?   The Mississippi.

2. What / tall / buildings in the world?

   _____   _____

3. What / crowded / cities in the world?

   _____   _____

4. What / famous / buildings in the world?

   _____   _____

5. What / polluted / places in the world?

   _____   _____

6. Who / good / athletes in the world?

   _____   _____

EXERCISE 4: The Comparative and Superlative Form of Adjectives

Write two sentences. Use the superlative form of the adjective in parentheses for one sentence. Use the comparative form for the other.

1. a train / a plane / a bus (fast)

   A plane is the fastest of the three.

   A train is faster than a bus.

2. a teenager / a child / a baby (old)

   _____

   _____

3. Nigeria / Spain / Sweden (hot)

   _____

   _____

4. a street / a path / a highway (wide)

   _____

   _____

5. a city / a village / a town (big)

   _____

   _____

6. an elephant / a gorilla / a fox (heavy)

   _____

   _____

7. an hour / a second / a minute (long)

   _____

   _____

8. boxing / golf / soccer (dangerous)

   _____

   _____

EXERCISE 5: Editing

Correct the conversation. There are six mistakes. The first mistake is already corrected. Find and correct five more.

A: My dog Topper is the ~~goodest~~ *best* dog in the world. A lot of my friends have dogs, but Topper is smartest.

B: Is she the most pretty too?

A: She's one of the prettiest. She's also the sweeter.

B: Is she sweeter than your old dog Spike?

A: Spike was sweet, but Topper is friendly with everyone. I think Topper is the friendliest dog of the neighborhood, and she's also one of the almost playful dog I know.

EXERCISE 6: Personal Writing

Write about your favorite animal. Use a superlative and **one of** *+ superlative.*

EXAMPLE: My favorite animal is the giraffe. It's the tallest animal in the world, and it's also one of the quietest. In fact, giraffes make no sounds at all. I love giraffes because they are so beautiful. I think they are the most graceful animals in the world. I love to watch them on TV. Hopefully, one day I will see them up close.

_____

_____

_____

_____

WORKBOOK ANSWER KEY

In this answer key, where the contracted form is given, the full form is often also correct, and where the full form is given, the contracted form is often also correct.

UNIT 1 (pages 1–5)

EXERCISE 1

2. is	**5.** are	**8.** is
3. am	**6.** is	**9.** is
4. is	**7.** are	**10.** am

EXERCISE 2

2. we	**6.** It	**10.** He
3. She	**7.** They	**11.** He
4. It	**8.** We	**12.** It
5. He	**9.** They	

EXERCISE 3

Answers will vary. Sentences with: I am / My best friend is / My mother is / My father is / My teacher is / My parents are / My classmates are

EXERCISE 4

2. Gwyneth Paltrow is not a tennis player. She is an actress.
3. Chris Martin is not Gwyneth Paltrow's neighbor. He is her husband.
4. Chris Martin is not an ice hockey player. He is a singer.
5. Dallas is not a state. It is a city.
6. California is not a country. It is a state.
7. Egypt and China are not cities. They are countries.
8. Boston and New York are not in Canada. They are in the United States.
9. Ottawa is not the capital of the United States. It is the capital of Canada.
10. Mexico is not in Central America. It is in North America.

EXERCISE 5

2. is	**5.** are	**8.** is not
3. is not	**6.** are not	**9.** are
4. are not	**7.** is	**10.** is not

EXERCISE 6

2. We are from New York. I am from New York too.
3. I am a big baseball fan. I am not.
4. Jessica is a very good soccer player. She is a good student too.

5. You are Mark, right? No, I am not Mark. I am his brother Mike.
6. Pedro is nineteen. No, he is not. He is sixteen.
7. Basketball is a popular sport. Soccer is popular too. They are not popular in my country.

EXERCISE 7

2. Yung-Hee and Ali aren't in class today. They're at a game.
3. The teacher's not in class. (OR The teacher isn't in class.) I know. She's sick.
4. Antonio's a student in your class. His name's not on my list. (OR His name isn't on my list.)
5. Melinda's successful. She's pretty too.
6. I'm right. No, you're not. (OR No, you aren't.) You're wrong.
7. They're my books. No, they're not. (OR No, they aren't.) They're my books.

EXERCISE 8

My favorite sport ~~are~~ *is* baseball. It ~~be~~ *is* popular in the United States. My favorite players are Felix Hernandez and Hanley Ramirez. ~~Are~~ *They are* baseball players in the United States. But they *are* not from the United States. Felix Hernandez ~~he~~ is from Venezuela. Hanley Ramirez is ~~no~~ *not* from Venezuela. He *is* from the Dominican Republic.

EXERCISE 9

Answers will vary.

UNIT 2 (pages 6–12)

EXERCISE 1

3. Are we in the right classroom?
4. Why are you and your classmates unhappy?
5. Who is your teacher?
6. We are very good students.
7. I am from Florida.
8. Is your watch expensive?
9. Where is Michigan?
10. Are the students from the same country?
11. Is your car comfortable?
12. This exercise is easy.

EXERCISE 2

2. f	**5.** l	**8.** k	**11.** a
3. h	**6.** c	**9.** i	**12.** b
4. j	**7.** g	**10.** e	

EXERCISE 3

Some answers will vary.

2. Are you happy? Yes, I am. (OR No, I'm not.)
3. Is your mother a student? Yes, she is. (OR No, she's not. OR No, she isn't.)
4. Is today Thursday? Yes, it is. (OR No, it's not. OR No, it isn't.)
5. Are your friends from California? Yes, they are. (OR No, they're not. OR No, they aren't.)
6. Is your friend talented? Yes, he / she is. (OR No, he's / she's not. OR No, he / she isn't.)
7. Are you a singer? Yes, I am. (OR No, I'm not.)
8. Is your teacher friendly? Yes, he / she is. (OR No, he's / she's not. OR No, he / she isn't.)
9. Are your mother and father Canadian? Yes, they are. (OR No, they're not. OR No, they aren't.)
10. Are you married? Yes, I am. (OR No, I'm not.)
11. Are your classmates young? Yes, they are. (OR No, they're not. OR No, they aren't.)
12. Is it eleven o'clock? Yes, it is. (OR No, it's not. OR No, it isn't.)

EXERCISE 4

3. Where are they from? Brazil.
4. Why is your mother in bed? Because she's tired.
5. What is in the bag? A sandwich.
6. Where is the post office? On Park Street.
7. Who is your favorite writer? Shakespeare.
8. How is your English class? It's great!
9. When is the class trip? On Saturday.
10. Why are you here? I'm your new teacher.

EXERCISE 5

2. Why	**4.** Why	**6.** Who
3. where	**5.** What	**7.** Where

EXERCISE 6

2. Where is (OR Where's) the hospital?
3. Who is (OR Who's) Javier Bardem?
4. Where is (OR Where's) Room 203?
5. Where are my keys?
6. Who is (OR Who's) (that) on the phone?
7. What are Cadillacs?
8. What is (OR What's) that?
9. Where is (OR Where's) the wastepaper basket?
10. How are your parents?

EXERCISE 7

CLAUDIA: Excuse me. ~~This is~~ *Is this* Room 202?

TEACHER: Yes, ~~it's~~ *it is*.

ENRIQUE: Oh. ~~We~~ *Are we* late for class?

TEACHER: No, you're right on time.

ENRIQUE: That's good!

TEACHER: So, what *are* your names? ~~You are~~ *Are you* Ana Leite and Fernando Romeiro from Brazil?

CLAUDIA: No, we're ~~are~~ not. I'm Claudia Rodriguez. And this is Enrique Montero. [OR *No, we aren't.*]

TEACHER: Where ~~you are~~ *are you* from?

CLAUDIA: We're from Venezuela.

TEACHER: Hmm . . . your names are not on my list. Are you in English 4?

CLAUDIA: No, I don't think. *so* I think we're in English 2.

TEACHER: Then this is not your class. You're in Room 302.

CLAUDIA: Who *is* the teacher ~~is~~?

TEACHER: I'm not sure.

EXERCISE 8

A.–B. *Answers will vary.*

UNIT 3 (pages 13–17)

EXERCISE 1

A. 2. was		**4.** were
3. were		**5.** was

B. 2. His work was not perfect. It was terrible!
3. His co-workers were not sad when he left. They were happy.
4. His customers were not happy with his work. They were unhappy.
5. He was not hardworking. He was lazy!

EXERCISE 2

3. William Shakespeare and Charles Dickens weren't Canadian.
4. Barack Obama wasn't the first president of the United States.
5. Charlie Chaplin and Marilyn Monroe were movie stars.
6. The end of World War I wasn't in 1942.
7. *Titanic* was the name of a movie.
8. Toronto and Washington, D.C., weren't big cities 300 years ago.

9. Indira Gandhi and Napoleon were famous people.
10. Nelson Mandela was a political leader.
11. Oregon and Hawaii weren't part of the United States in 1776.
12. Disneyland wasn't a famous place 100 years ago.

EXERCISE 3

Answers will vary.

2. Were you a student 10 years ago? Yes, I was. (OR No, I wasn't.)
3. Were you in English class yesterday? Yes, I was. (OR No, I wasn't.)
4. Were all the students in class last week? Yes, they were. (OR No, they weren't.)
5. Was the weather nice yesterday? Yes, it was. (OR No, it wasn't.)
6. Was your teacher at work two days ago? Yes, he / she was. (OR No, he / she wasn't.)

EXERCISE 4

2. What were you? (OR What was your first job?)
3. Where was your store?
4. How was your job?
5. How were your co-workers?
6. When were you at the drugstore?

EXERCISE 5

3. is	9. is	15. were
4. is	10. was	16. was
5. is	11. was	17. were
6. are	12. were	18. were
7. is	13. Were	19. Are
8. Is	14. were	20. are

EXERCISE 6

A: So how ~~your first day in class was~~? *was your first day in class*

B: It ~~weren't~~ too good at first. *wasn't*

A: What ~~is~~ wrong? *was*

B: First, I ~~no was~~ in the right classroom. Two other students ~~was~~ in the wrong classroom too. The class was boring. Everything was so difficult. *wasn't* *were*

A: How long ^ you there? *were*

B: For half an hour.

EXERCISE 7

Answers will vary.

UNIT 4 (pages 18–22)

EXERCISE 1

3. clothes	8. holiday
4. photos	9. teeth
5. umbrella	10. hat
6. erasers	11. artist
7. scissors	12. earrings

EXERCISE 2

3. They're clothes.	8. It's a holiday.
4. They're photos.	9. They're teeth.
5. It's an umbrella.	10. It's a hat.
6. They're erasers.	11. It's an artist.
7. They're scissors.	12. They're earrings.

EXERCISE 3

2. Javier Bardem **a.**	6. Yo-Yo Ma **c.**
3. Elizabeth II **e.**	7. Hillary Clinton **b.**
4. Lady Gaga **h.**	8. J. K. Rowling **g.**
5. Neil Armstrong **f.**	

EXERCISE 4

2. Javier Bardem is an actor.
3. Elizabeth II is a queen.
4. Lady Gaga is a singer.
5. Neil Armstrong is an astronaut.
6. Yo-Yo Ma is a musician.
7. Hillary Clinton is a politician.
8. J. K. Rowling is an author.

EXERCISE 5

/s/— notebooks, roommates, states, students
/z/—dictionaries, girls, lemons, sons
/iz/—boxes, classes, houses, watches

EXERCISE 6

3. men	7. continents	11. universities
4. songs	8. states	12. watches
5. cities	9. countries	13. actors
6. rivers	10. holidays	14. mountains

EXERCISE 7

2. 2 children, 3 children
3. 6 teeth, 7 teeth
4. 1 foot, 4 feet
5. 1 grandchild, 7 grandchildren
6. 1 person, 9 people
7. 2 sisters-in-law, 3 sisters-in-law

EXERCISE 8

This is _a photo of me and my sister. Isn't she
striking? She's _{an} architect. She lives in ~~miami~~ _{Miami} with
her husband and two ~~childs~~ _{children}. He's a ~~dentists~~ _{dentist}. In this
photo, my sister and I are at a special party for our
_{parents} ~~parent~~.

EXERCISE 9

Answers will vary.

UNIT 5 (pages 23–26)

EXERCISE 1

2. difficult	**7.** comfortable
3. boring	**8.** ugly
4. expensive	**9.** old
5. safe	**10.** warm
6. small	

EXERCISE 2

2. It is a long movie.
3. The Prado is a famous museum.
4. You are an unusual photographer.
5. They are interesting buildings.
6. He is an intelligent man.
7. It is a crowded village.
8. She is a popular soccer player.
9. We are good students.
10. This is an easy exercise.

EXERCISE 3

Answers will vary.
2. It is / isn't famous.
3. It is / isn't an awesome place.
4. The people are / aren't friendly.
5. The buildings are / aren't unusual.
6. It is / isn't an expensive city.
7. It is / isn't a crowded place.
8. There is / isn't a beautiful park.

EXERCISE 4

2. They are beautiful carpets.
3. Those hotels are expensive.
4. They are honest men.
5. They are tall girls.
6. Eggs are white or brown.
7. They are good actors.
8. These watches are cheap.
9. They are interesting stories.
10. The summers are hot and dry.

EXERCISE 5

Answers will vary.

UNIT 6 (pages 27–30)

EXERCISE 1

Answers will vary.

EXERCISE 2

2. between	**5.** in	**8.** in
3. next to	**6.** near	**9.** next to
4. near	**7.** between	**10.** near

EXERCISE 3

2. in	**5.** On	**8.** on
3. In	**6.** on	**9.** on
4. in	**7.** At	**10.** in

EXERCISE 4

A: Where are you?
B: Near ~~to~~ the ABC Movie Theater.
A: ~~At~~ _{On} Water Avenue?
B: Yeah, the corner _{of} Water Avenue and Park Street. Where are you?
A: I'm ~~on~~ _{at} the museum. It's right next ~~of~~ _{to} City Hall.
B: Oh, OK. Where in the museum?
A: ~~In~~ _{On} the second floor, between the cafeteria and the stairs, in front of the sculpture exhibit.

EXERCISE 5

Answers will vary.

UNIT 7 (pages 31–37)

EXERCISE 1

A. **2.** e	**5.** a		**8.** j
3. b	**B.** **6.** i		**9.** f
4. c	**7.** g		**10.** h

EXERCISE 2

3. Clean	**7.** Don't be	**11.** Don't use
4. Don't talk	**8.** Don't tell	**12.** Don't touch
5. Don't buy	**9.** Study	
6. Ask	**10.** Give	

EXERCISE 3

2. Get off	**4.** turn	**6.** make
3. Go (OR Walk)	**5.** Walk (OR Go)	**7.** Ring

EXERCISE 4

2. b	**5.** a	**8.** a
3. b	**6.** a	**9.** a
4. a	**7.** b	**10.** b

EXERCISE 5

A. 2. Let's get something to eat.

　3. Let's go swimming.

　4. Let's not invite her to the party.

B. 5. Why don't we go out and look for him?

　6. Why don't we go inside?

　7. Why don't we leave?

EXERCISE 6

A. 2. e　　　**4.** a

　3. b　　　**5.** d

B. 6. (*Possible answer*) Why don't you turn on the TV?

　7. (*Possible answer*) Why don't you watch movies in English?

　8. (*Possible answer*) Why don't you take an aspirin?

EXERCISE 7

2. don't, it	**5.** OK
3. Why, instead	**6.** plan
4. Sorry, can't	**7.** Sounds

EXERCISE 8

Let's
A: ~~Let~~ go for a walk. It's a beautiful afternoon.

don't
B: That's a good idea. Why ~~not~~ we walk to Fireside and get something to eat?

A: Which restaurants are open there in the afternoon?

Look　　　　　*don't*
B: I don't know. ~~You look~~ online, but ~~not~~ take a long time. I'm ready to go.

A: How about Chico's?

B: That sounds good. But let's ~~to~~ call first. They're usually crowded.

Give
A: OK. ~~You are give~~ me the phone.

EXERCISE 9

Answers will vary.

UNIT 8 (pages 38–42)

EXERCISE 1

2. They're secretaries.	**6.** You're a cook.
3. He's a pilot.	**7.** He's a mechanic.
4. She's a professor.	**8.** She's a doctor.
5. They're flight attendants.	

EXERCISE 2

2. teaches	**5.** plays	**8.** paint
3. sings	**6.** manages	**9.** washes
4. dances	**7.** collect	**10.** fight

EXERCISE 3

2. take	**11.** has	**19.** isn't
3. goes	**12.** is	**20.** helps
4. has	**13.** doesn't have	**21.** are
5. live	**14.** live	**22.** go
6. don't live	**15.** studies	**23.** is
7. have	**16.** works	**24.** don't have
8. don't live	**17.** leaves	**25.** try
9. is	**18.** doesn't come	**26.** don't get
10. lives		

EXERCISE 4

2. Water doesn't boil at 90° C. It boils at 100° C.

3. Water doesn't freeze at 5° C. It freezes at 0° C.

4. The Earth doesn't go around the moon. The Earth goes around the sun.

5. Penguins don't come from the Arctic. They come from the Antarctic.

6. Cows don't eat meat. They eat grass.

7. China doesn't have a small population. It has a big population.

8. Deserts don't have a lot of water. They have a lot of sand.

9. Elephants don't have small ears. They have big ears.

10. Egypt doesn't have a cold climate. It has a hot climate.

11. The sun doesn't shine at night. It shines during the day.

12. Cats don't run after dogs. Cats run after mice.

EXERCISE 5

look
A: Those pants ~~looks~~ cute on you.

don't
B: Really? I ~~no~~ like them very much.

like
A: Oh, I ~~likes~~ them a lot. And they go well with

cost
the shirt. It's a nice outfit. And it doesn't ~~costs~~ much, only $45.

has
B: Hmm . . . I'm not sure. My brother ~~have~~ a shirt

don't
like this. I ~~doesn't~~ want the same thing.

goes
A: What about this shirt? It ~~go~~ well with the pants too.

doesn't
B: I don't know. It ‸look like my style.

EXERCISE 6

Answers will vary.

UNIT 9 (pages 43–47)

EXERCISE 1

2. A	**5.** C	**8.** A	**11.** D
3. D	**6.** B	**9.** C	**12.** C
4. A	**7.** D	**10.** B	

EXERCISE 2

2. f	**4.** a	**6.** g	**8.** d
3. c	**5.** b	**7.** h	

EXERCISE 3

3. Yes, she does.
4. No, she doesn't.
5. Yes, they do.
6. Yes, she does.
7. No, they don't.
8. No, he doesn't.
9. Yes, they do.
10. No, they don't.

EXERCISE 4

3. doesn't	**6.** don't	**9.** don't
4. doesn't	**7.** don't	**10.** doesn't
5. don't	**8.** don't	

EXERCISE 5

2. Does he have
3. Do they like
4. Do you live
5. Does he know
6. Do you want
7. Do you have
8. Does she wear
9. Do you like
10. Do you know
11. Do they work
12. Does he come

EXERCISE 6

2. Does your roommate ~~likes~~ *like* your girlfriend?
3. ~~The~~ *Does the* teacher wear glasses?
4. ~~Do~~ *Does* Mr. Flagg have a car?
5. ~~Does~~ *Do* your roommates always sleep late?
6. *Does* Peter eat fast?
7. ~~Are~~ *Does* she leave for work at the same time every day?
8. ~~Is~~ *Does* loud music bother you?
9. Does the doctor ~~has~~ *have* your telephone number?
10. ~~Football~~ *Do football* players play in the summer?

EXERCISE 7

Answers will vary.

UNIT 10 (pages 48–52)

EXERCISE 1

3. Where		**8.** Where
4. What		**9.** When
5. Who		**10.** Why
6. When		**11.** How
7. Who		**12.** When

EXERCISE 2

2. What do you have for breakfast? Cereal.
3. How do you feel after a nap? Great.
4. Who corrects your homework? My teacher.
5. Where does Rosita work? At City Central Bank.
6. When do you and your family go on vacation? In August.
7. What do you wear to work? A suit and tie.
8. Why do you need more money? Because I want to buy a new computer.
9. What time do the kids eat lunch? At noon.
10. When does the mail come? In the morning.
11. Where does Doug play soccer? At his school.
12. Who does Mark visit on Sundays? His friends.

EXERCISE 3

2. How		**6.** When
3. Why		**7.** why
4. What		**8.** what
5. Where		

EXERCISE 4

2. b	**4.** a	**6.** b	**8.** a
3. a	**5.** a	**7.** b	

EXERCISE 5

2. Why do you drink tea at night?
3. What do you remember about your dream?
4. How does your roommate look in the morning?
5. Why do teenagers sleep late?
6. Where does your roommate sleep?
7. Who (usually) wakes you up?
8. When do you sleep late?
9. Who sleeps in the small bedroom?
10. What do you do after your nap?
11. Who sleeps a lot in your family?
12. When does she wake up?

EXERCISE 6

A: ~~How~~ *How often* do you have nightmares?

B: Not very often. Maybe once a year. But unfortunately, my son has nightmares frequently.

does he dream
A: What ~~dreams he~~ about?

B: We're not sure. He wakes up crying during the night.

goes
A: Who ~~does go~~ to his room?

B: Sometimes I do. Sometimes my husband does. Or sometimes he runs into our room.

do
A: What ‸you tell him?

B: Different things.

have
A: Why does he ~~has~~ nightmares?

B: Because he's afraid of a lot of different things.

does he
A: How ~~he does~~ feel in the morning?

B: He never remembers anything.

EXERCISE 7

Answers will vary.

UNIT 11 (pages 53–61)

EXERCISE 1

3. there are	**6.** There are	**9.** There is
4. There is	**7.** there is	**10.** there is
5. there are	**8.** There are	

EXERCISE 2

2. There is a computer in the store.
3. There are two restaurants on the first floor.
4. There are people at the door.
5. There is an amusement park near the mall.
6. There is a bookstore between the cafés.
7. There is an international market on the second floor.
8. There are boxes on the floor.
9. There are five children near the man and woman.

EXERCISE 3

3. There is a clock for sale.
4. There is a bicycle for sale.
5. There is a bed for sale.
6. There are televisions for sale.
7. There are balls for sale.
8. There are hats for sale.
9. There are books for sale.
10. There are suitcases for sale.
11. There are shoes for sale.
12. There are lamps for sale.
13. There are CDs for sale.

EXERCISE 4

3. There are two beds in every room.
4. There are two closets in every room.
5. There isn't a telephone in every room.
6. There is a television in every room.
7. There is an air conditioner in every room.
8. There isn't a refrigerator in every room.
9. There isn't a swimming pool at the hotel.
10. There are two restaurants at the hotel.
11. There are four tennis courts at the hotel.
12. There aren't gift shops at the hotel.
13. There are two parking lots at the hotel.

EXERCISE 5

3. There are two banks. They are on Main Street.
4. There are three clothing stores. They aren't very expensive.
5. There aren't any bookstores.
6. There are four drugstores. They are small.
7. There are three gas stations. They are in the center of town.
8. There aren't any hospitals.
9. There aren't any movie theaters.
10. There are two restaurants. They are open for lunch and dinner.
11. There are three schools. They aren't far from Main Street.
12. There are two supermarkets. They are big.
13. There aren't any indoor swimming pools.

EXERCISE 6

2. Yes, there are.	**6.** No, there aren't.
3. No, there aren't.	**7.** No, there aren't.
4. Yes, there are.	**8.** No, there aren't.
5. Yes, there are.	**9.** Yes, there are.

EXERCISE 7

2. Are there many elephants in India? Yes, there are.
3. Is there a desert in Canada? No, there isn't.
4. Are there camels in Saudi Arabia? Yes, there are.
5. Is there a long river in the Sahara Desert? No, there isn't.
6. Are there many lions in Russia? No, there aren't.
7. Are there mountains in Kenya? Yes, there are.
8. Are there many people in Antarctica? No, there aren't.
9. Is there a big city in Thailand? Yes, there is.
10. Is there a monkey in your garden? No, there isn't.

EXERCISE 8

2. there	**6.** there's	**10.** they're
3. It's	**7.** It's	**11.** There's
4. There's	**8.** There are	**12.** She's
5. there	**9.** They're	

EXERCISE 9

A: ~~There is~~ *Is there* a food court in the mall?

B: Yes, ~~it~~ is. There is *there* on the second floor. There ~~is~~ *one* eight or ten places with different kinds of food.

A: Is ~~it~~ *there* a place with Chinese food?

B: I think so. But there ~~isn't~~ *aren't* any with Japanese food.

A: What about pizza places? Are there any?

B: No, but there ~~are~~ *is* a great pizza place next to the mall. They have all kinds of pizza and ~~there~~ *they* are delicious.

EXERCISE 10

Answers will vary.

UNIT 12 (pages 62–72)

EXERCISE 1

2. Mrs. Simpson's
3. Mary Rose's
4. Nora's
5. Bill's
6. Joe Mott's
7. Dr. Lin's
8. Maria Lico's
9. Tom Cho's

EXERCISE 2

Subject Pronoun	Object Pronoun	Possessive Adjective	Possessive Pronoun
I	me	my	mine
you	you	your	yours
he	him	his	his
she	her	her	hers
it	it	its	X
we	us	our	ours
they	them	their	theirs

EXERCISE 3

2. your, their
3. her, his
4. our, their
5. my, her
6. your, his, my (OR our), Her

EXERCISE 4

2. He, His
3. She, her
4. They, Their, their, It
5. We, Our
6. I, I, My
7. She, Her
8. We, Our, Its, It, it
9. Their, They, They

EXERCISE 5

3. Mariana's their neighbor.
4. Her last name is Martinez.
5. She's an aunt.
6. Danny and Frederico are her nephews.
7. He's eight years old.
8. His eyes are blue.
9. Her dogs are always outside.
10. He's afraid of the dogs.
11. They were with their aunt yesterday.
12. She was with her dogs.
13. Their food was in the garage.
14. They were in the garage.
15. Their friends were not with them yesterday.
16. They were happy to be with their aunt.

EXERCISE 6

3. correct
4. correct
5. Please bring me my car.
6. Where is her car?
7. correct
8. correct
9. We need our car.
10. Their car is expensive.
11. correct
12. Why do you want your car?

EXERCISE 7

3. his
4. ours
5. Yours
6. theirs
7. his
8. hers
9. Theirs
10. ours

EXERCISE 8

2. my, yours, mine
3. hers, hers
4. our, ours
5. Their, their, theirs
6. his, his

EXERCISE 9

3. Whose eggs are these?
4. Whose bananas are these?
5. Whose bread is this?
6. Whose potatoes are these?
7. Whose cake is this?
8. Whose milk is this?
9. Whose orange juice is this?
10. Whose potato chips are these?
11. Whose carrots are these?
12. Whose bag is this?

EXERCISE 10

2. She loves him.
3. They love us.
4. We love them.
5. I know you.
6. You don't know her.

EXERCISE 11

2. us	**6.** you	**10.** him
3. them	**7.** her	**11.** them
4. you	**8.** them	**12.** him
5. her	**9.** us	

EXERCISE 12

2. It, it	**5.** I, me	**7.** we, us
3. she, her	**6.** they, them	**8.** you
4. him, He		

EXERCISE 13

2. Our, We, us	**6.** your, Yours, You
3. We, ours, our	**7.** It, it, Its
4. me, my, I	**8.** their, theirs, them
5. His, his, him	**9.** her, She, hers

EXERCISE 14

2. **A:** What's Ms. ~~Baker~~ *Baker's* first name?
   B: It's Sandra.
3. **A:** Where's the ~~men~~ *men's* room?
   B: It's over there. Do you see ~~its~~ *it*?
4. **A:** Whose handwriting is this?
   B: It's ~~my~~ *mine*.
5. **A:** Are your ~~brothers~~ *brothers'* wives friendly?
   B: Yes, I like ~~her~~ *them* very much.
6. **A:** ~~Who's~~ *Whose* books are these? Are they yours or Miriam's?
   B: They're hers.
7. **A:** I can't find my teacher.
   B: Look in the ~~teachers~~ *teachers'* lunchroom. Many teachers are in there.
8. **A:** Where are Elena and Sam?
   B: They're not here, but ~~theirs~~ *their* bags are in the back of the room.

EXERCISE 15

Answers will vary.

EXERCISE 1

2. farm worker	**3.** driver	**4.** secretary

EXERCISE 2

4. can drive and lift 100 pounds.
5. can type and speak Spanish.
6. can control animals, use heavy equipment, and work long days.
7. can't type, and he can't speak Spanish.
8. can't drive, and she can't lift 100 pounds.
9. can control animals and work long days, but she can't use heavy equipment.
10. can manage dogs, but he can't walk long distances.
11. can drive, but he can't lift 100 pounds.
12. can speak Spanish, but she can't type.

EXERCISE 3

2. Can your mother lift 100 pounds? Yes, she can. (OR No, she can't.)
3. Can your father play the guitar? Yes, he can. (OR No, he can't.)
4. Can your best friend ride a horse? Yes, he / she can. (OR No, he / she can't.)
5. Can your parents speak Spanish? Yes, they can. (OR No, they can't.)
6. Can you swim? Yes, I can. (OR No, I can't.)
7. Can you type? Yes, I can. (OR No, I can't.)
8. Can your parakeet talk? Yes, he / she / it can. (OR No, he / she / it can't.)
9. Can your dog do tricks? Yes, he / she / it can. (OR No, he / she / it can't.)
10. Can your cat catch mice? Yes, he / she / it can. (OR No, he / she / it can't.)

EXERCISE 4

2. could practice	**7.** couldn't get
3. couldn't go	**8.** could hear
4. couldn't answer	**9.** couldn't go
5. couldn't eat	**10.** could do
6. could play	

EXERCISE 5

A: So how was dog training class? Can Charlie ~~to do~~ *do* any new tricks?

B: Nope. He's just not as intelligent as the other dogs. They can ~~doing~~ *do* lots of tricks but Charlie can't.

A: Like what?

B: Well, he ~~no can~~ [*can't*] roll over. All of the other dogs

could ~~did~~ [*do*] that in yesterday's class, but not Charlie.

A: What else ~~the other dogs can~~ [*can the other dogs*] do?

B: They can get the newspaper and bring it back.

A: That's strange. Charlie ~~can~~ [*could*] do that last week. He did it for me.

EXERCISE 6

Answers will vary.

UNIT 14 (pages 78–81)

EXERCISE 1

2. b	**4.** b	**6.** b	**8.** a
3. b	**5.** a	**7.** a	**9.** b

EXERCISE 2

2. pay by credit card **5.** sit here
3. come in **6.** bring my boyfriend
4. speak to the doctor

EXERCISE 3

2. Can I (OR May I) open the window?
3. Can I (OR May I) use the telephone?
4. Can I (OR May I) get a ride (with you)?
5. Can I (OR May I) use (OR borrow) your eraser?
6. Can I (OR May I) have a drink of water?
7. Can I (OR May I) ask you a question?
8. Can I (OR May I) sit at the empty table in the corner?

EXERCISE 4

RECEPTIONIST: Can I ~~be~~ help you?

BOB: May I ~~seeing~~ [*see*] the nurse? I don't feel well.

RECEPTIONIST: Yes, ~~may you~~ [*you may*] go in. The nurse's office is the first door on the right.

[15 minutes later.]

NURSE: Here, take this medicine twice a day.

BOB: May I ~~takes~~ [*take*] some now?

NURSE: No, wait until dinnertime.

BOB: When ~~I can go~~ [*can I go*] back to class? May I ~~be~~ go tomorrow?

NURSE: No, wait until next week. You can go back to class then.

EXERCISE 5

Answers will vary.

UNIT 15 (pages 82–88)

EXERCISE 1

2. e	**4.** a	**6.** c	**8.** f	**10.** i
3. b	**5.** j	**7.** g	**9.** h	

EXERCISE 2

3. smiling	**9.** run	**15.** begin
4. shining	**10.** holding	**16.** reading
5. rain	**11.** talk	**17.** cry
6. make	**12.** hoping	**18.** staying
7. sleeping	**13.** doing	
8. listening	**14.** put	

EXERCISE 3

3. right now	**6.** these days	**9.** right now
4. right now	**7.** these days	**10.** these days
5. these days	**8.** these days	

EXERCISE 4

2. aren't standing, are sitting
3. is watching, isn't reading
4. aren't reading, are reading
5. isn't running, is standing
6. is holding, isn't talking
7. is buying, isn't buying
8. are smiling, aren't crying

EXERCISE 5

3. I am (OR am not) having a good time.
4. The sun is (OR is not) shining.
5. It is (OR is not) raining.
6. It is (OR is not) getting dark.
7. I am (OR am not) listening to the radio.
8. I am (OR am not) talking on the phone.
9. I am (OR am not) sitting on a chair.
10. My neighbors are (OR are not) making a lot of noise.

EXERCISE 6

2. is snowing	**7.** am writing
3. are skiing	**8.** are making
4. are relaxing	**9.** are enjoying
5. are sitting	**10.** is playing
6. is reading	

EXERCISE 7

How are you doing?

                                     I'm not
I'm in between classes right now, so ~~I no am~~ doing
        sitting
anything. I'm ~~sit~~ in the school cafeteria. All the other
           are   *I'm*
people around me ~~is~~ eating, but I'm not hungry. ~~I~~
just having a cup of coffee and thinking about my
classes.
        taking   *We're*
I'm ~~take~~ some good classes this semester. ~~We~~
doing lots of interesting things, but the classes are
tough. Also, there's no time for extra-curricular
          getting
activities. I'm not ~~get~~ good grades, so I'm a little
worried, especially about my math class. But my
          are
classmates and I studying hard for our next math
test. We study together every Tuesday and Thursday,
and it's helping me a lot.

Anyway, that's the news from here.

EXERCISE 8

Answers will vary.

UNIT 16 (pages 89–97)

EXERCISE 1

2. Are you wearing glasses? Yes, I am. (OR No, I'm not.)
3. Is your English teacher correcting papers? Yes, he / she is. (OR No, he's / she's not. OR No, he / she isn't. OR I don't know.)
4. Are you and a friend watching a movie? Yes, we are. (OR No, we're not. OR No, we aren't.)
5. Are your classmates doing this exercise now? Yes, they are. (OR No, they're not. OR No, they aren't. OR I don't know.)
6. Are you having dinner with your neighbors? Yes, I am. (OR No, I'm not.)
7. Is the sun shining? Yes, it is. (OR No, it's not. OR No, it isn't. OR I don't know.)
8. Are your friends waiting for you? Yes, they are. (OR No, they're not. OR No, they aren't. OR I don't know.)
9. Are your parents working? Yes, they are. (OR No, they're not. OR No, they aren't. OR I don't know.)
10. Are you coughing? Yes, I am. (OR No, I'm not.)
11. Is your teacher helping you? Yes, he / she is. (OR No, he's / she's not. OR No, he / she isn't.)
12. Are the children playing outside? Yes, they are. (OR No, they're not. OR No, they aren't. OR I don't know.)

EXERCISE 2

2. Who	4. Where	6. Where
3. Why	5. What	7. Who

EXERCISE 3

2. Is she sleeping?
3. Are they playing?
4. Are they swimming?
5. Is he getting money?
6. Are they having a good time?
7. Is she visiting someone?
8. Are they playing tennis?
9. Is she fixing something?
10. Is he coming?
11. Are they waiting for me?
12. Is he following me?

EXERCISE 4

2. Why are you watching an old movie?
3. What are the people talking about?
4. Who is Kevin meeting?
5. Where are they meeting?
6. Why are they meeting at the mall?
7. Who is laughing?
8. What are they laughing about?
9. Where are you sitting?
10. What are you eating?

EXERCISE 5

2. Who is Kevin meeting?
3. What are you and Kevin doing?
4. What are you eating?
5. What are the people talking about?
6. Why are they meeting at the mall?
7. What are they laughing about?
8. Where are you sitting?
9. Who is laughing?
10. Where are they meeting?

EXERCISE 6

2. a	4. a	6. b
3. b	5. b	7. a

EXERCISE 7

2. What are you reading?
3. Why are they coughing?
4. What is he cooking?
5. Who's coming?
6. Why are you going to bed?
7. Where are you going?
8. Why are you selling your car?
9. Where are they swimming?
10. What are you watching?
11. Who are they watching?
12. Who is she dating?

EXERCISE 8

A: Are you ~~watch~~ *watching* the game?

B: No, I'm watching an old movie. This is one of my favorite scenes.

A: ~~What~~ *What's* happening? Who ˄ the people ~~are~~ *are* waiting for?

B: They're all standing around and waiting for the wizard.

A: Who's standing in the middle? Is she the wizard?

B: No, she is waiting for the wizard. She needs his help. Look, here he comes now.

A: What ˄ *is* he wearing? ~~He is~~ *Is he* wearing pajamas?

B: No, he's not ~~wearing~~ ˄. Those are his special clothes. They give him special powers.

A: This is a stupid movie. Can we change the channel and watch the game?

EXERCISE 9

Answers will vary.

UNIT 17 (pages 98–103)

EXERCISE 1

2. a	**5.** c	**8.** h	**11.** j
3. b	**6.** f	**9.** l	**12.** g
4. e	**7.** k	**10.** d	

EXERCISE 2

2. drives buses, is driving
3. fixes cars, is fixing
4. serves food, is serving
5. paint pictures, are painting
6. do experiments, are doing
7. write articles, are writing
8. cuts meat, is cutting
9. counts money, is counting
10. bake bread and cake, are baking
11. waters plants and flowers, is watering
12. feeds animals, is feeding

EXERCISE 3

3. have, non-action verb
4. have, action verb
5. know, non-action verb
6. are . . . packing, action verb
7. need, non-action verb
8. 'm writing, action verb
9. flies, action verb
10. Do . . . send, action verb

11. looks, non-action verb
12. looks, action verb
13. owe, non-action verb
14. visit, action verb
15. are, non-action verb

EXERCISE 4

2. a	**6.** b	**10.** a	**13.** b
3. b	**7.** a	**11.** a	**14.** a
4. a	**8.** b	**12.** b	
5. a	**9.** a		

EXERCISE 5

2. don't care	**14.** don't think
3. Do you want	**15.** has
4. 's playing	**16.** 's doing
5. don't know	**17.** hear
6. don't have	**18.** 's talking
7. 's raining	**19.** 's talking
8. have	**20.** doesn't understand
9. don't have	**21.** 's getting
10. don't need	**22.** do you know
11. is	**23.** know
12. like	**24.** don't know
13. wants	

EXERCISE 6

ALAN: Hi, Marsha. This is Alan. What ~~do you do~~ *are you doing* right now?

MARSHA: Oh, hi, Alan. ~~I cut~~ *I'm cutting* some vegetables for dinner.

ALAN: ~~Are~~ *Do* you ~~preparing~~ *prepare* dinner at this time every evening?

MARSHA: Yeah, usually. We ~~are eating~~ *eat* dinner at around 8:00 or 8:30. Why? When do you have dinner?

ALAN: Oh, my family and I ~~are eating~~ *eat* much earlier. The kids are ~~being~~ usually hungry by 6:30 or 7:00.

MARSHA: Really? Our kids ~~are having~~ *have* a snack at 5:00. Then they're not hungry until 8:00. So, what's up?

ALAN: Listen. ~~I work~~ *I'm working* on a report for the office, and there is a problem. ~~Are you having~~ *Do you have* a couple of minutes to talk about it?

MARSHA: Sure.

EXERCISE 7

Answers will vary.

UNIT 18 (pages 104–109)

EXERCISE 1

2. i **4.** e **6.** b **8.** f
3. a **5.** g **7.** c **9.** h

EXERCISE 2

2. Last **4.** Yesterday **6.** yesterday
3. Last **5.** yesterday **7.** last

EXERCISE 3

a.–c. *Answers will vary.*
2. Karen learned how to drive _____ years ago.
3. Karen visited her high school friends _____ months ago.
4. Karen called her grandparents _____ days ago.
5. Karen talked to her parents _____ days ago.
6. Karen shared an apartment with friends _____ years ago.
7. Karen traveled to Hong Kong _____ months ago.
8. Karen invited some friends for dinner _____ days ago.
9. Karen worked in Miami _____ years ago.
10. Karen started her own business _____ months ago.

EXERCISE 4

2. They played basketball
3. She washed her clothes
4. They studied
5. He worked in his garden
6. He picked up his daughter after school
7. She talked to her son
8. They traveled to France
9. It closed at 3:00 P.M.
10. They watched TV

EXERCISE 5

2. enjoyed, didn't enjoy
3. emailed, didn't email
4. landed, didn't land
5. promised, didn't promise
6. visited, didn't visit
7. tried, didn't try
8. walked, didn't walk
9. canceled, didn't cancel
10. rented, didn't rent

EXERCISE 6

I arrived at the hotel at ten o'clock ~~the~~ last night. I *enjoyed* ~~enjoy~~ the flight, but the plane didn't ~~landed~~ *land* on time. This morning we walked around the town. (We *did* not rent a car because it was very expensive.) I *tried* ~~try~~ to speak Spanish to some of the people in the stores, but they didn't understand me. ~~Ago a few hours~~ *A few hours ago* we ~~did~~ visited a very famous park and *listened* ~~listen~~ to some great musicians. We're having a really good time so far.

EXERCISE 7

Answers will vary.

UNIT 19 (pages 110–113)

EXERCISE 1

3. put, irregular, put
4. had, irregular, have
5. brushed, regular, brush
6. left, irregular, leave
7. arrived, regular, arrive
8. began, irregular, begin
9. learned, regular, learn
10. finished, regular, finish
11. met, irregular, meet
12. ate, irregular, eat
13. went, irregular, go
14. stayed, regular, stay

EXERCISE 2

2. got **7.** said **12.** taught
3. ate **8.** knew **13.** left
4. put **9.** met **14.** bought
5. went **10.** came **15.** began
6. had **11.** sold

EXERCISE 3

Probable answers
2. I didn't eat 3 kilos of oranges for breakfast yesterday morning.
3. I didn't sleep 21 hours yesterday.
4. I didn't bring a horse to English class two weeks ago.
5. I didn't go to the moon last month.
6. I didn't meet the leader of my country last night.
7. I didn't find $10,000 in a brown paper bag yesterday.
8. I didn't do this exercise two years ago.
9. I didn't swim 30 kilometers yesterday.
10. I didn't speak English perfectly 10 years ago.

EXERCISE 4

2. didn't get	**10.** ate	**18.** didn't have
3. got	**11.** took	**19.** drove
4. went	**12.** stayed	**20.** saw
5. met	**13.** looked	**21.** invited
6. went	**14.** bought	**22.** didn't eat
7. didn't see	**15.** didn't buy	**23.** watched
8. didn't have	**16.** came	**24.** didn't leave
9. closed	**17.** made	

EXERCISE 5

          became
Barack Obama ~~become~~ the 44th president of the
                was
United States in January 2009. He born in Hawaii
in 1961. His father was Kenyan, and his mother
              met
was American. They ~~meet~~ at the University of Hawaii
and got married, but they didn't stay married for a
long time. After his parents divorced, his mother
              took
married a man from Indonesia and ~~taked~~ her son to
live in Jakarta from the age of six to ten. Then he
           spent
returned to Hawaii. He ~~spended~~ a lot of time with
his grandparents. He graduated from high school
          go
in 1979, but he didn't ~~went~~ to college in Hawaii. He
 left
~~leaved~~ Hawaii in 1979 to attend college in California,
                    went
but he stayed there only two years. Then he ~~go~~ to
Columbia University in New York and graduated
from there in 1983.

EXERCISE 6

Answers will vary.

UNIT 20 (pages 114–120)

EXERCISE 1

2. Yes, he did.	**6.** Yes, he did.
3. Yes, he did.	**7.** No, she didn't.
4. No, they didn't.	**8.** No, he didn't.
5. Yes, he did.	

EXERCISE 2

Answers will vary.

3. Did you buy food for dinner?
4. got
5. Did you meet Glen for lunch?
6. ate
7. Did you write a letter to Rena?
8. mailed
9. Did you go to the bank?

10. deposited
11. Did you return the book to the library?
12. took
13. Did you look for a birthday present for Jane?
14. bought
15. Did you call the doctor?
16. said
17. Did you bake some cookies?
18. have
19. Did you pick the children up at 4:00?
20. forgot

EXERCISE 3

2. f	**4.** g	**6.** a	**8.** h
3. b	**5.** i	**7.** d	**9.** c

EXERCISE 4

2. When did a person walk on the moon for the first time? In 1969.
3. What did J. K. Rowling write? The *Harry Potter* books.
4. Where did the Olympic Games start? In Greece.
5. Why did many people go to California in 1849? They wanted to find gold.
6. How long did Bill Clinton live in the White House? Eight years.
7. What did Alfred Hitchcock make? Movies.
8. Why did the Chinese build the Great Wall? They wanted to keep foreigners out of the country.
9. How long did World War II last in Europe? About six years.
10. When did Christopher Columbus sail to America? In 1492.

EXERCISE 5

2. Who gave	**7.** Who did she send
3. Who did you see	**8.** Who cleaned
4. Who called	**9.** Who did she marry
5. Who wrote	**10.** Who did they stay
6. Who took	

EXERCISE 6

            did you
A: What movie ~~you did~~ see?
B: I went to see *Invictus*.
          starred
A: Who ~~did star~~ in it?
B: Matt Damon and Morgan Freeman.
A: Who directed it?
B: Clint Eastwood.
          was
A: What ~~did~~ it ~~be~~ about?
B: It was about Nelson Mandela and his relationship with the coach of the Springboks, the national rugby team of South Africa.

did it take
A: When ~~it took~~ place?
B: In the 1990s, after Mandela became president of South Africa.
like
A: Did you ~~liked~~ the movie?
B: Yes, I did ~~like~~. My husband liked it too, especially the rugby games.

EXERCISE 7

Answers will vary.

UNIT 21 (pages 121–128)

EXERCISE 1

2. made	**5.** didn't have	**8.** didn't eat
3. left	**6.** didn't play	**9.** watched
4. were	**7.** bought	

EXERCISE 2

2. No, they weren't. (OR Yes, they were.)
3. Yes, I did. (OR No, I didn't.)
4. Yes, he was. (OR No, he wasn't.)
5. Yes, it was. (OR No, it wasn't.)
6. Yes, I did. (OR No, I didn't.)
7. Yes, I was. (OR No, I wasn't.)
8. No, they didn't. (OR Yes, they did.)
9. Yes, we did. (OR No, we didn't.)
10. Yes, it was. (OR No, it wasn't.)
11. Yes, he / she did. (OR No, he / she didn't.)
12. Yes, I was. (OR No, I wasn't.)

EXERCISE 3

2. Were you good at history in school? Yes, it was my favorite subject.
3. Were your history books interesting? They were OK.
4. Were you a talkative child? No, I was very quiet.
5. Were your parents born in the United States? No, they were born in Colombia.
6. Was your mother born in 1942? Yes, she was born in May 1942.
7. Was Michael Jordan a great baseball player? No, he was a great basketball player.
8. Was the movie about Ray Charles good? Yes, the actor was outstanding.

EXERCISE 4

2. b	**4.** b	**6.** a	**8.** b	**10.** a
3. a	**5.** a	**7.** b	**9.** b	

EXERCISE 5

2. was, h	**6.** did, c	**10.** did, f
3. did, i	**7.** was, a	**11.** did, j
4. was, b	**8.** was, l	**12.** was, d
5. did, g	**9.** were, k	

EXERCISE 6

2. were you
3. was it
4. were they afraid
5. was the score
6. was the name of the store
7. were they born
8. were they here
9. were you with (OR was with you)
10. was Eleanor Roosevelt

EXERCISE 7

did
A: Where ~~you~~ grow up?
was   *did*
B: In Montreal. I ~~am~~ born in Morocco, but I not live there for a long time, only two years.
like
A: Did you ~~liked~~ life in Montreal?
wasn't
B: I loved it. It was home. But it ~~not be~~ easy for my parents. They always missed life in Morocco, especially the weather.
did
A: Why ~~were~~ you move to New York?
got
B: I went to college here and then I ~~get~~ a job, so I
go
didn't ~~went~~ back to Canada.
A: Where are your parents now?
ago
B: My father died ~~before~~ five years, and my mother is back in Morocco with her sisters.

EXERCISE 8

Answers will vary.

UNIT 22 (pages 129–131)

EXERCISE 1

2. g	**4.** i	**6.** c	**8.** e
3. f	**5.** b	**7.** a	**9.** d

EXERCISE 2

2. Terry hates traveling (OR to travel).
3. Marsha loves taking (OR to take) photographs.
4. Elena loves writing (OR to write) poems.
5. Steve enjoys being on an airplane.
6. Dana enjoys speaking other languages.
7. Rena hates to work (OR working) in an office.
8. Leo enjoys learning new things.

EXERCISE 3

2. to swim (OR swimming)
3. to help
4. to talk
5. to move
6. to be
7. to receive (OR receiving)
8. to do (OR doing)
9. to relax
10. studying

EXERCISE 4

A: Are you thinking about ~~go~~ *going* to graduate school?

B: Yes, I want *to* be a software developer, so I need to get a master's degree.

A: Where do you plan ~~working~~ *to work*?

B: I don't know. I'm getting tired of ~~live~~ *living* here, so I'm thinking about moving to Chicago.

A: Why Chicago?

B: I was born there, and I always enjoy ~~to visit~~ *visiting* the city. What about you? What are your plans?

A: Oh, I don't know. I avoid ~~to think~~ *thinking* about the future.

EXERCISE 5

Answers will vary.

UNIT 23 (pages 132–136)

EXERCISE 1

1. 'm living, have, ate
2. had, don't go, 's
3. are you doing, told, listen
4. moved, don't live, 'm writing
5. gave, use, make

EXERCISE 2

2. Scientists are coming up with new ways to use these medicines.
3. I slept well last night.
4. She rejected all of our ideas.
5. They're inventing new uses for the phone.

EXERCISE 3

2. I'm not thinking about their plans for the future.
3. The teacher doesn't give homework every day.
4. We didn't accept all of their suggestions.
5. They didn't discover a cure for that disease.

EXERCISE 4

1. has, got, does, is cleaning
2. am writing, forgot, Do you remember
3. am waiting, comes, arrived, was
4. was, hurt, is, is examining, sees, went
5. are having, eat, were, didn't come
6. are looking, is getting, doesn't start, is, didn't start, took

EXERCISE 5

A: I ~~am wanting~~ *want* to pay for these things.

B: ~~Do you pay~~ *Are you paying* with cash or a credit card?

A: Credit. Here's my card.

B: You ~~forget~~ *forgot* to sign the back of it.

A: Really? I didn't know that. I ~~am~~ *was* using it just a few minutes ago and the cashier ~~doesn't~~ *didn't* say anything.

B: Oh, people ~~are doing~~ *do* it all the time.

EXERCISE 6

Answers will vary.

UNIT 24 (pages 137–146)

EXERCISE 1

2. The professors are going to give their opinion about the plans this evening.
3. The students are probably going to protest the plans tomorrow evening.
4. The architects are going to present new plans for the campus next week.
5. The workers are going to start work on the new building next month.
6. A story about new buildings on campus is going to be on TV tonight.
7. We are going to take a tour of the new arts center this afternoon.

EXERCISE 2

2. Max is going to leave the office in 15 minutes.
3. Max and Debbie are going to get married in six months.
4. Debbie is going to start a new job in two weeks.
5. Debbie is going to take Max to her parents' home in four days.

EXERCISE 3

Answers will vary.

EXERCISE 4

Possible answers

I am (OR am not) going to study tomorrow.
I am (OR am not) going to go shopping tomorrow.
I am (OR am not) going to take pictures tomorrow.
I am (OR am not) going to watch TV tomorrow.
I am (OR am not) going to go out with friends tomorrow.
I am (OR am not) going to listen to music tomorrow.
I am (OR am not) going to visit relatives tomorrow.
I am (OR am not) going to talk on the telephone tomorrow.
I am (OR am not) going to take a shower tomorrow.
I am (OR am not) going to check my email tomorrow.
I am (OR am not) going to go skiing tomorrow.
I am (OR am not) going to stay home tomorrow.

EXERCISE 5

Possible answers

2. She's going to drive.
3. They're going to take a trip.
4. They're going to take pictures.
5. He's going to watch a movie.
6. He's going to study.

EXERCISE 6

2. She isn't (OR She's not) going to take
3. She isn't (OR She's not) going to take
4. They aren't (OR They're not) going to play
5. They aren't (OR They're not) going to watch
6. I'm not going to eat
7. We aren't (OR We're not) going to swim
8. He isn't (OR He's not) going to see
9. I'm not going to wake up
10. He isn't (OR He's not) going to deliver

EXERCISE 7

2. Who is going to cook tonight?
3. When is dinner going to be ready?
4. Why is he going to cook so much food?
5. How long is he going to need to cook the dinner?
6. Who is going to come?
7. How is he going to cook the lamb?
8. Where are all of your guests going to sit?
9. What are you going to do?
10. How long are your guests going to stay?

EXERCISE 8

2. What is he going to make?
3. Why is he going to cook so much food?
4. How is he going to cook the lamb?
5. Who is going to come?

6. How long is he going to need to cook the dinner?
7. What are you going to do?
8. When is dinner going to be ready?
9. How long are your guests going to stay?
10. Where are all of your guests going to sit?

EXERCISE 9

3. 'm doing, now
4. 're having, future
5. 're moving, future
6. Are having, now
7. Are leaving, future
8. are sleeping, now
9. are going, future
10. is coming, now

EXERCISE 10

2. They are flying to London at 7:30 on May 8.
3. They are arriving in London at 6:45 A.M. on May 9.
4. They are staying at the London Regency Hotel on May 9 and 10.
5. They are visiting Buckingham Palace at 2:00 P.M. on May 9.
6. They are having tea at the Ritz Hotel at 4:30 on May 9.
7. They are going to the theater at 7:30 on May 9.
8. They are going on a tour of central London at 9:00 A.M. on May 10.
9. They are eating lunch at a typical English pub at 12:00 P.M. on May 10.
10. They are leaving for Scotland at 8:00 A.M. on May 11.

EXERCISE 11

2. Are you going shopping this weekend? Yes, I am. (OR No, I'm not.)
3. Are you working next week? Yes, I am. (OR No, I'm not.)
4. Is your friend having a party next Saturday? Yes, he / she is. (OR No, he's / she's not. OR No, he / she isn't.)
5. Are your classmates studying with you tonight? Yes, they are. (OR No, they're not. OR No, they aren't.)
6. Is your neighbor coming to your place tomorrow? Yes, he / she is. (OR No, he's / she's not. OR No, he / she isn't.)
7. Are your parents moving next year? Yes, they are. (OR No, they're not. OR No, they aren't.)
8. Are your classmates having dinner together tomorrow? Yes, they are. (OR No, they're not. OR No, they aren't.)
9. Are you and your friends going to the movies on the weekend? Yes, we are. (OR No, we're not. OR No, we aren't.)
10. Is your teacher making lunch for you tomorrow? Yes, he / she is. (OR No, he's / she's not. OR No, he / she isn't.)

EXERCISE 12

2. When are you leaving?
3. How are you getting there? (or How are you going?)
4. Why are you driving?
5. How long are you staying?
6. Who are you going with?
7. What are you taking?

EXERCISE 13

A: *Is the*
~~The~~ mayor going to meet with the police chief this morning?

B: No, he isn't ~~going~~. *He's going* ~~He goes~~ to meet with the Parents' and Teachers' Association. They're going to talk about conditions in the schools.

Then he's going to ~~having~~ *have* lunch with a group of community leaders.

A: What ~~they are~~ *are they* going to discuss?
B: I don't know. But they aren't ~~being~~ happy with the budget for next year. There's going ^*to* be less money for all the neighborhood centers!

EXERCISE 14

Answers will vary.

UNIT 25 (pages 147–153)

EXERCISE 1

2. I'll get you some water.
3. I'll help you.
4. I'll turn on the air conditioner.
5. I'll make you a sandwich.
6. I'll get you some aspirin.
7. I'll drive you.
8. I'll wash them.

EXERCISE 2

2. Scientists will find cures for many diseases. We won't get sick as often.
3. Many more people will live to be 100 years old. They'll also be healthier.
4. We won't use paper money and coins for our purchases. We'll use credit cards.
5. Robots will cook our meals and clean our homes. We'll have a lot more leisure time.
6. Cars will run on solar energy. They won't use gasoline.
7. Travel to the moon will be common. We'll go to the moon on vacation!

EXERCISE 3

2. You'll be very happy there. / You won't be very happy there.
3. I'll be there early. / I won't be there early.
4. She'll do it. / She won't do it.
5. It'll be hot tomorrow. / It won't be hot tomorrow.
6. They'll come to the meeting. / They won't come to the meeting.
7. He'll get the job. / He won't get the job.

EXERCISE 4

2. a	4. a	6. b	8. a
3. b	5. a	7. b	9. b

EXERCISE 5

2. I won't leave late.
3. It won't be hot (or warm).
4. Coffee won't cost more.
5. People won't spend less time with their families.
6. We won't come before seven o'clock.
7. Mr. and Mrs. McNamara won't buy a new car.
8. Valerie won't lose the game.
9. The parking lot won't be full.

EXERCISE 6

2. Will I be	11. won't be
3. will marry	12. will bother
4. will I meet	13. won't like
5. will be	14. Will our home have
6. Will she love	15. won't leave
7. will we meet	16. won't bother
8. won't have	17. will become
9. will be	18. Will that make
10. will I be	

EXERCISE 7

2. took	9. don't sit
3. was	10. don't lie
4. ate	11. 'll be
5. wasn't	12. 'll return
6. are resting	13. won't be
7. aren't sitting	14. 'll be
8. aren't lying	

EXERCISE 8

A: Things will ~~are~~ *be* different next year.
B: How will ~~be they~~ *they be* different?
A: Well, for one thing, I won't ~~be~~ be in school any more. I won't ~~takes~~ *take* any more exams, and I'll have lots of free time.
B: Will you have a job?

A: Yes, ~~I'll~~. *I will* I hope to have a very good job.

B: Then how will you *have* lots of free time?

A: It'll be a different kind of free time.

EXERCISE 9

Answers will vary.

EXERCISE 1

Answers will vary.

EXERCISE 2

2. They may (OR might) not listen to the weather report.
3. He may (OR might) not drive in the snow.
4. They may (OR might) stay home.
5. She may (OR might) go to the beach.
6. We may (OR might) not ride our bikes in the hot weather.
7. You may (OR might) need a hat.
8. There may (OR might) be flooding on the highway.
9. The weather report may (OR might) be wrong.
10. The weather may (OR might) improve.

EXERCISE 3

3. may	**5.** will	**7.** may	**9.** will
4. will	**6.** may	**8.** will	**10.** may

EXERCISE 4

3. may (OR might) have an accident.
4. may (OR might) break.
5. may (OR might) not win.
6. may (OR might) get lost.
7. may (OR might) not live.
8. may (OR might) bite.
9. may (OR might) get sick.
10. may (OR might) close.

EXERCISE 5

A: ~~Maybe I go~~ *I may go* to the movies tonight.

B: Take your umbrella. It may ~~rains~~ *rain*. What are you going to see?

A: I don't know. ~~I'll~~ *I might* OR *may* see the new Sam Fong movie. I heard good things about it. Do you want to come?

B: I can't. I'm waiting for a call from Dana. We might ~~be~~ study together tonight.

A: On a Saturday night?

B: It's the only free time I have. I ~~mightn't~~ *might not* be around next week.

A: Why? Where ~~may~~ *will* you be?

B: Working in my father's store. He might have to go in the hospital for a few days, but we're not sure yet.

EXERCISE 6

Answers will vary.

EXERCISE 1

2. 5	**6.** 8	**10.** 4	**14.** 8
3. 7	**7.** 4	**11.** 5	**15.** 3
4. 1	**8.** 1	**12.** 7	
5. 9	**9.** 8	**13.** 2	

EXERCISE 2

Count Nouns—eggs, vegetables, napkins, bags, potato chips, toothbrushes
Non-Count Nouns—ice cream, fruit, milk, rice, food, bread, fish

EXERCISE 3

Circled Nouns—furniture, money, information, rain, oil, people, uncle, cell phone, questions, computer
Count Nouns—a student, some teeth, some children, some friends, an animal, some people, an uncle, some questions, a computer, a cell phone
Non-Count Nouns—some water, some paper, some homework, some advice, some traffic, some furniture, some money, some information, some rain, some oil

EXERCISE 4

2. a	**5.** a	**8.** b	**10.** a
3. a	**6.** a	**9.** b	**11.** b
4. a	**7.** a		

EXERCISE 5

2. a	**5.** a	**7.** the, The
3. the	**6.** the, a	**8.** a, a, a
4. the		

EXERCISE 6

3. He bought some orange juice.
4. He didn't buy any lemons.
5. He bought a newspaper.
6. He didn't buy any bread.
7. He didn't buy any onions.
8. He didn't buy a toothbrush.
9. He bought some potatoes.
10. He didn't buy any lettuce.
11. He didn't buy any carrots.
12. He bought some butter.
13. He bought some milk.
14. He bought some eggs.

EXERCISE 7

Answers will vary.

a lot of / any—food in my refrigerator, money
in my pocket, books next to my bed, shirts in my
closet, friends, free time, children, work to do today,
questions for my teacher, jewelry, medicine in my
bathroom, problems with my English grammar,
photographs in my wallet, ice cream at home

a little / much—cheese in my pocket, food in my
refrigerator, money in my pocket, free time, work
to do today, jewelry, medicine in my bathroom, ice
cream at home

a few / many—books next to my bed, shirts in my
closet, friends, children, questions for my teacher,
problems with my English grammar, photographs in
my wallet

EXERCISE 8

A: How did you like ~~a~~ *the* restaurant?

B: ~~Atmosphere~~ *The atmosphere* was nice, but the food wasn't great.
I had some fish but it didn't have ~~some~~ *any* sauce, so
it was very dry. Gerry had some roast beef, but
it had ~~much~~ *a lot of* salt. She didn't eat much of it.

A: Did you have ~~the~~ dessert?

B: Yes, that was delicious. There were ₍*a*₎ lot of
choices on the menu. I had ~~any~~ *some* almond cake.
Gerry had ₍*some*₎ banana ice cream with a small
banana cupcake. She loved the dessert.

A: Was the restaurant crowded?

B: There were a ~~little~~ *few* people, but for a Saturday
night it was pretty empty.

EXERCISE 9

Answers will vary.

EXERCISE 1

A. 2. d   B. 5. g   8. e   11. j
   3. a   6. h   C. 9. l   12. i
   4. c   7. f   10. k

EXERCISE 2

3. One carton.
4. Two heads.
5. Three (bottles).
6. One (box).
7. Four rolls.
8. Three bars.
9. One tube.
10. Two (jars).

EXERCISE 3

3. How much flour do you need?
4. How much sugar do you have?
5. How many bananas do you want?
6. How many oranges do you want?
7. How much cereal do you need?
8. How many potatoes do you need?
9. How much milk do you want?
10. How many roses do you want?
11. How many cookies do you have?
12. How much money do you have?

EXERCISE 4

2. is (OR is not) enough television.
3. is (OR is not) enough fruit.
4. is (OR is not) enough spinach.
5. is (OR is not) enough water.
6. is (OR is not) enough sleep.

EXERCISE 5

Answers will vary.

EXERCISE 6

2. How often does Donna eat out? She frequently
eats out.
3. How often does David cook? He never cooks.
4. How often do Barbara and Ed eat out? They
never eat out.
5. How often does Ed have dessert? He often has
dessert.
6. How often does Barbara cook? She cooks three
times a week.
7. How often do Barbara and David have dessert?
They rarely have dessert.
8. How often do Ed and George cook? They cook
once or twice a week.
9. How often do George and David eat out? They
eat out almost every day.
10. How often does George have dessert? He almost
never has dessert.

11. How often does Donna have dessert? She has dessert every day.
12. How often does Ed drink coffee? He never drinks coffee.

EXERCISE 7

A: How ~~many~~ *much* bread pudding do you want?

B: Just a little bit. Hmm. This is delicious.

A: I don't think it has ~~sugar enough~~ *enough sugar*.

B: Really? I think it's perfect. So how often *do* you cook?

A: I ~~cook usually~~ *usually cook* every day. My wife doesn't like to cook, but I do.

B: Well, she's lucky. So how do you make this bread pudding? How many different ingredients does it have?

A: Oh, it's pretty easy. All you need are 12 ~~slice~~ *slices* of bread, some eggs, some vanilla, butter, sugar, and one cup of milk.

B: How ~~much~~ *many* eggs do you need?

A: Four.

EXERCISE 8

Answers will vary.

UNIT 29 (pages 173–178)

EXERCISE 1

2. too crowded
3. too old
4. too hot
5. too heavy
6. too expensive
7. too big
8. too young

EXERCISE 2

2. There are too many days.
3. There are too many numbers.
4. There is too much water.
5. There is too much furniture.
6. There is too much food.
7. There are too many birds.
8. There is too much shampoo.
9. There are too many cars.
10. There is not enough toothpaste.
11. There is not enough air.
12. There are not enough chairs.

EXERCISE 3

3. There were too few people for two teams.
4. We had too little paper for everyone in the class.
5. There was too little food for 15 people.
6. You have too little information.
7. There are too few bedrooms in that apartment.
8. We had too little time for the test.
9. There are too few bananas for a banana cake.
10. There are too few salesclerks at that store.

EXERCISE 4

2. b	5. a	8. a
3. a	6. b	9. b
4. b	7. b	10. a

EXERCISE 5

A: I can't hear you. There's too ~~many~~ *much* noise. What did you say?

B: How do you like your new neighborhood?

A: It's too ~~much~~ noisy. There are too ~~much~~ *many* cars and too ~~little~~ *few* parking places.

B: Are there places for the children to play?

A: No, there are too *few* parks. There's only one.

B: How's the apartment?

A: It's not too small, but it costs too ~~little~~ *much* money.

EXERCISE 6

Answers will vary.

UNIT 30 (pages 179–184)

EXERCISE 1

2. shouldn't	5. shouldn't	8. shouldn't
3. should	6. should	9. should
4. shouldn't	7. should	10. shouldn't

EXERCISE 2

2. I ought to look up information about the country on the Internet.
3. Business people ought to learn about the customs of other countries.
4. The visitor ought to bring a gift.
5. We ought to be careful.
6. To avoid confusion, you ought to put the date on your paperwork.

EXERCISE 3

2. I should learn how to speak the language.
3. Ms. Jones should put her email address on her business card.
4. You should plan your trip carefully.
5. The students should ask more questions.
6. We should avoid making that gesture; people consider it an insult.

EXERCISE 4

2. should look for another one.
3. shouldn't smoke.
4. should go to the dentist.
5. should wash it.
6. shouldn't leave a tip.
7. should study more.
8. should leave early.
9. shouldn't watch it.
10. shouldn't touch it.

EXERCISE 5

2. Why should we have
3. How many (people) should we invite
4. Who should we invite
5. What should we buy
6. What should we cook
7. Where should we get
8. What should we do
9. When should we send

EXERCISE 6

2. a	5. a	8. e
3. e	6. c	9. d
4. d	7. b	10. b

EXERCISE 7

2. had better not serve shrimp
3. had better get a couple of bottles
4. had better not let the dog in the house
5. had better ask Costas to bring her
6. had better not sit together at the table
7. had better invite him
8. had better rent a video
9. had better borrow some from the neighbors

EXERCISE 8

      had
A: You ~~have~~ better not wear that to the reception. You should ~~to~~ wear something more formal.
      wear
B: Should I ~~wearing~~ this?
A: Yeah. I think that's better. And you ought to wear a tie.

      had better
B: Really? Then I ~~better had~~ change my shoes.
    Should I
    ~~Ought I to~~ wear these brown ones?
A: No, I think the black ones are better.
      should I
B: What time ~~I should~~ leave?
A: Soon. You don't want to be late.

EXERCISE 9

Answers will vary.

UNIT 31 (pages 185–190)

EXERCISE 1

1. At a bus station.
3. At a movie theater.
2. On an airplane.

EXERCISE 2

3. The teacher would like to see you.
4. Would the children like hamburgers or hot dogs?
5. Would you like to check your email on my computer?
6. Would Paul like to come to the party?
7. My husband would like rice with his fish.
8. Neil and Jane would like a bigger apartment.
9. Would you like to have a cup of coffee with me?
10. We would like to go home now.

EXERCISE 3

2. Would you like
3. Would you like
4. would like / 'd like
5. Would you like
6. what would you like to do
7. Where would you like to go
8. Would you like to go
9. Would you like to see
10. What time would you like to go
11. would like to get / 'd like to get
12. Where would you like to eat

EXERCISE 4

2. Would (OR Could) you please give me the key to my room?
3. Would (OR Could) you please explain the meaning of the word *selfish*?
4. Would (OR Could) you please give me change for a dollar?
5. Would (OR Could) you please take a picture of me and my friends?
6. Would (OR Could) you please take me to the airport?
7. Would (OR Could) you please lend me a hand with my suitcases?

8. Would (OR Could) you please show me the brown shoes in the window?
9. Would (OR Could) you please sit down?

EXERCISE 5

2. a   **3.** a   **4.** b   **5.** a   **6.** a

EXERCISE 6

      Would
A: ~~Do~~ you like some help?
B: Yes, thank you. Could you ⨯ lend me a hand with these boxes?
     Sure.   *do*
A: ~~Yes, I could.~~ So how ~~would~~ you like the building?
             I'd
B: I like it a lot, but ~~I~~ like to meet the neighbors. I don't know many people yet.
A: Would you like to come to my party tonight? A lot of the neighbors will be there.
B: That sounds great . . . Well, I think that's all the boxes. Would you like some coffee?
A: No, ~~I wouldn't like any,~~ thank you. See you tonight at 8. Apartment 3F.

EXERCISE 7

Answers will vary.

UNIT 32 (pages 191–198)

EXERCISE 1

Answers will vary.

EXERCISE 2

2. have to, don't have to
3. don't have to, have to
4. have to, don't have to
5. don't have to, have to
6. have to, don't have to
7. don't have to, have to
8. have to, don't have to
9. have to, don't have to
10. don't have to, have to

EXERCISE 3

2. has to leave early today
3. have to go food shopping today
4. have to take a taxi
5. doesn't have to work late today
6. don't have to clean up their room
7. has to take some medicine
8. don't have to pay for the tickets
9. has to wear a suit and tie this morning
10. doesn't have to do housework

EXERCISE 4

2. I don't have to write everything 10 times.
3. The teacher didn't have to come early yesterday.
4. One student had to stay after class yesterday.
5. I don't have to check my email every day.
6. My friends didn't have to work last week.
7. The school has to have clean classrooms.
8. The teacher doesn't have to work on the weekend.
9. Students have to have a 75 percent average to pass that course.
10. I have to write down the new words.

EXERCISE 5

2. You must stop.
3. You mustn't turn right.
4. You mustn't turn left.
5. You mustn't drive faster than 55 mph.
6. You mustn't park in this area.
7. You mustn't make a U-turn.
8. You mustn't pass.
9. You must go more slowly.

EXERCISE 6

2. They had to find someone to take care of their dog.
3. They had to get to the airport on time.
4. They didn't have to get up early every morning.
5. They didn't have to go to work.
6. They had to look for a hotel.
7. They didn't have to make the bed every morning.
8. They had to pack and unpack suitcases.
9. They had to pay their hotel bill.
10. They didn't have to wash dishes.

EXERCISE 7

2. Does your mother have to get up at six o'clock in the morning? Yes, she does. (OR No, she doesn't.)
3. Did you have to cook last night? Yes, I did. (OR No, I didn't.)
4. Does your best friend have to do this exercise? Yes, he / she does. (OR No, he / she doesn't.)
5. Do you have to be in English class on time? Yes, I do. (OR No, I don't.)
6. Do your friends have to learn English? Yes, they do. (OR No, they don't.)
7. Did your father have to shave yesterday? Yes, he did. (OR No, he didn't.)
8. Did your best friend have to go to work yesterday? Yes, he / she did. (OR No, he / she didn't.)
9. Did you have to take a test last week? Yes, I did. (OR No, I didn't.)

EXERCISE 8

2. does she have to take a test?
3. does he have to leave early?
4. did the students have to wait for their teacher?
5. did you have to meet after class?
6. does the teacher have to talk to?

7. did he have to pay for the class?
8. does she have to buy?
9. do you have to finish your paper?
10. did the schools have to close?

EXERCISE 9

A: You mustn't ~~to~~ talk to your neighbor during the exam. You have to be quiet and ~~have to~~ work fast. You have only one hour for the exam.

B: Excuse me? ~~Have we~~ *Do we have* to use a pencil?

A: No, you don't ~~have~~. You can use a pencil or a pen.

C: Excuse me? Can I use my electronic dictionary during the exam?

A: No, you have ~~put~~ *to* put everything away. You ~~don't have to~~ *mustn't* have anything on your desks except the exam. Any more questions? OK. We must get started.

EXERCISE 10

Answers will vary.

UNIT 33 (pages 199–202)

EXERCISE 1

✓—2, 5, 10

EXERCISE 2

One Syllable—fast, high, hot, long, old, small
Two Syllables—crowded, diverse, easy, friendly, heavy, messy, noisy, pretty
Three or Four Syllables—dangerous, expensive, intelligent

EXERCISE 3

2. more beautiful
3. milder
4. bigger
5. more diverse
6. farther
7. more intelligent
8. worse
9. messier
10. more comfortable
11. more careful
12. prettier
13. more difficult
14. easier
15. better

EXERCISE 4

2. longer than
3. more expensive than
4. bigger than
5. higher than
6. hotter than
7. more dangerous than
8. more crowded than
9. noisier than
10. heavier than
11. faster than
12. friendlier than

EXERCISE 5

Answers to the questions will vary.

3. Is this book cheaper or more expensive than your notebook?
4. Is your country bigger or smaller than Canada?
5. Is your English pronunciation better or worse than last year?
6. Which is healthier, coffee or tea?
7. Which is nicer, dinner at home or dinner in a restaurant?

EXERCISE 6

A: I'm thinking about moving to Brighton. Apartments there are ~~more~~ cheaper.

B: Brighton will be less convenient. It is ~~more far~~ *farther* from your job.

A: Yeah, but not a lot. I can take the highway, so my commute won't be much ~~long~~ *longer*.

B: They highway is busier ~~from~~ *than* the small streets you use now.

A: But there are no traffic lights on the highway. Besides, I don't go to work until 10 A.M. The traffic is ~~badder~~ *worse* from 7 to 9.

B: Well, I hope you find a nice place. It's probably ~~more easy~~ *easier* to find something now.

EXERCISE 7

Answers will vary.

UNIT 34 (pages 203–206)

EXERCISE 1

3. adjective
4. adjective
5. adverb
6. adjective
7. adverb
8. adverb
9. adverb
10. adjective
11. adjective
12. adverb
13. adverb
14. adjective
15. adverb

EXERCISE 2

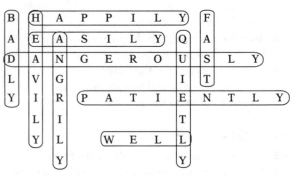

EXERCISE 3

2. quietly
3. dangerously
4. angrily
5. happily
6. well
7. badly
8. fast
9. patiently
10. easily

EXERCISE 4

2. good, good
3. fast, fast
4. tired, tired
5. angry, angrily
6. careful, carefully
7. easy, easily
8. bad, badly
9. serious, seriously

EXERCISE 5

A: How was the food at the reception? Did it taste
good
~~well~~?

B: Yeah, it was pretty good. But the service was
bad
~~badly~~. And after the meal, we had to listen to two more speeches. The first speaker spoke very
fast
~~fastly~~, and the second spoke very slowly.

A: Were they interesting speeches?

B: Not really. The speakers didn't know their
well
audience ~~good~~. The topics of the speeches
boring
sounded good, but the speeches were ~~boringly~~.
carefully
And I was tired, so I didn't listen very ~~careful~~.

EXERCISE 6

Answers will vary.

UNIT 35 (pages 207–215)

EXERCISE 1

2. h
3. g
4. a
5. b
6. f
7. e
8. d

EXERCISE 2

2. The questions are too difficult to answer.
3. The shirt is too small to wear.
4. It is too hot (OR warm) outside to go running.
5. The store is too far to walk.
6. The soup is too cold to eat.

EXERCISE 3

2. The story wasn't interesting enough.
3. Your room isn't neat (OR clean) enough.
4. Your hair isn't short enough.
5. You aren't old enough to watch that kind of TV program.
6. The numbers aren't big enough to see.

EXERCISE 4

2. too
3. too
4. very, too
5. very
6. too
7. very
8. very
9. too

EXERCISE 5

2. That cell phone is too expensive to buy.
3. I'm too tired to wait.
4. The steak was too tough (for Sandra) to eat.
5. Jeffrey isn't old enough to drive.
6. They aren't good enough to play on the team.
7. The tea is too hot to drink.
8. She's smart enough to do the work.

EXERCISE 6

3. too frightened
4. not big enough
5. too late
6. hot enough
7. too tight
8. too short
9. not safe enough
10. warm enough
11. not sunny enough

EXERCISE 7

✓—2, 3, 4, 6, 7

EXERCISE 8

3. as
4. than
5. as
6. than
7. as
8. as
9. as
10. than
11. than
12. than

EXERCISE 9

4. Trains aren't as fast as airplanes.
5. January is as cold as February.
6. The chair is as comfortable as the sofa.
7. The governor of Oregon isn't as famous as the president of the United States.
8. The bank isn't as far as the post office.
9. Limes are as sour as lemons.
10. Jazz is more relaxing than rock music.
11. Chocolate ice cream isn't as good as vanilla ice cream.
12. Some people are more violent than other people.
13. College isn't as easy as high school.
14. These boxes are as heavy as those boxes.

EXERCISE 10

2. Are you the same height as your brother?
3. Is your mother the same age as your father?
4. Is the dining room the same size as the living room?
5. Are the apples the same price as the pears?
6. Are you the same weight as your brother?
7. Is *War and Peace* the same length as *Crime and Punishment*?
8. Is the subway station the same distance as the bus stop?

EXERCISE 11

3. A bike is the same as a bicycle.
4. A TV is the same as a television.
5. North America is different from the United States.
6. 10,362 is different from 10.362.
7. 3 × 16 is the same as 16 × 3.
8. 16 ÷ 3 is different from 3 ÷ 16.
9. $1 is different from £1.
10. A snack bar is different from a restaurant.
11. 12:00 P.M. is the same as noon.
12. A plane is the same as an airplane.

EXERCISE 12

A: That black jacket isn't ~~enough big~~ *big enough*.
B: Really? It feels comfortable enough.
A: It doesn't look good on you. How about this green jacket? It is the same price ~~from~~ *as* that one.
B: But it isn't ^*as* warm as this black jacket. I want something that is ~~too~~ *very* warm.
A: There are some other jackets over there. They don't look very different ~~than~~ *from* the black one.
B: Hmm. . . . This one is as ~~nicer~~ *nice* as the black one, but it doesn't have ~~pockets enough~~ *enough pockets*.
A: So you want a warm jacket with lots of pockets.
B: Exactly. And one that isn't too small for me ^*to* wear.

EXERCISE 13

Answers will vary.

UNIT 36 (pages 216–219)

EXERCISE 1

2. Shanghai Garden
3. The Big Oven
4. Donnelly's
5. Circo
6. Circo
7. The Big Oven

EXERCISE 2

2. the worst
3. the hardest
4. the most beautiful
5. the busiest
6. the funniest
7. the best
8. the ugliest
9. the most popular
10. the lowest
11. the fastest
12. the most charming

EXERCISE 3

Answers to the questions will vary.

2. What is one of the tallest buildings in the world?
3. What is one of the most crowded cities in the world?
4. What is one of the most famous buildings in the world?
5. What is one of the most polluted places in the world?
6. Who is one of the best athletes in the world?

EXERCISE 4

2. A teenager is the oldest of the three.
   A child is older than a baby.
3. Nigeria is the hottest of the three.
   Spain is hotter than Sweden.
4. A highway is the widest of the three.
   A street is wider than a path.
5. A city is the biggest of the three.
   A town is bigger than a village.
6. An elephant is the heaviest of the three.
   A gorilla is heavier than a fox.
7. An hour is the longest of the three.
   A minute is longer than a second.
8. Boxing is the most dangerous of the three.
   Soccer is more dangerous than golf.

EXERCISE 5

A: My dog Topper is the ~~goodest~~ *best* dog in the world. A lot of my friends have dogs, but Topper is ^*the* smartest.
B: Is she the ~~most pretty~~ *prettiest*, too?
A: She's one of the prettiest. She's also the ~~sweeter~~ *sweetest*.
C: Is she sweeter than your old dog Spike?
A: Spike was sweet, but Topper is friendly with everyone. I think Topper is the friendliest dog ~~of~~ *in* the neighborhood, and she's also one of the ~~almost playful dog~~ *most playful dogs* I know.

EXERCISE 6

Answers will vary.